PIQUE YOUR PATH TO ACHIEVEMENTS

*P*rioritisation *I*nnovation *Q*ualification

ABBOUD BEJJANI

PIQUE YOUR PATH TO ACHIEVEMENTS

*Prioritisation Innovation
Qualification*

ABBOUD BEJJANI

PIQue Your Path to Achievements
Copyright © 2024 Abboud Bejjani
First published in 2024

Print: 978-1-76124-153-6
E-book: 978-1-76124-154-3
Hardback: 978-1-76124-159-8

All rights reserved. No part of this book may be reproduced, stored in a retrieval system, or transmitted by any means (electronic, mechanical, photocopying, recording, or otherwise) without written permission from the author.

Because of the dynamic nature of the Internet, any web addresses or links contained in this book may have changed since publication and may no longer be valid. The information in this book is based on the author's experiences and opinions. The views expressed in this book are solely those of the author and do not necessarily reflect the views of the publisher; the publisher hereby disclaims any responsibility for them.

The author of this book does not dispense any form of medical, legal, financial, or technical advice either directly or indirectly. The intent of the author is solely to provide information of a general nature to help you in your quest for personal development and growth. In the event you use any of the information in this book, the author and the publisher assume no responsibility for your actions. If any form of expert assistance is required, the services of a competent professional should be sought.

Publishing information
Publishing and design facilitated by Passionpreneur Publishing
A division of Passionpreneur Organization Pty Ltd
ABN: 48640637529

Melbourne, VIC | Australia
www.PassionpreneurPublishing.com

'**PIQ**ue' to stimulate interest or curiosity.

'Path' denotes a way or course taken in achieving something.

'Achievements' refer to things accomplished, especially through merit or effort.

'Pique Your Path to Achievements' means stimulating or invigorating your journey towards your goals and accomplishments. It suggests sparking interest or passion in the route you take to realise your achievements.

PIQ: Prioritisation Innovation Qualification

CONTENT

Dedication	ix
Acknowledgments	xi
Introduction: Charting the Uncharted Path	1
Chapter 1 My Journey: From Lebanon's Battlefront to Business Frontiers	7
Chapter 2 Success is a Life Journey: Navigating the Dynamic Interplay of Skills & Behaviour for Sustainable Achievements & Fulfilment	17
Chapter 3 Setting Your Priorities: Paving the Way to Success	27
Chapter 4 Find your Magic Road: We all need a Bit of Magic	49
Chapter 5 Realising the Best Version of Yourself: A Guide to Personal Excellence	67
Chapter 6 The Power Shift: Looking at Globalisation from a Different Perspective	89

Chapter 7	Love & Work: Creating a sharing environment while taking the first step	107
Chapter 8	Competition	135
Chapter 9	Philosophy-Driven Strategy	145
Chapter 10	Conclusion	165
Author Bio		167

DEDICATION

Dedicated to my late father and mother, who guided my path and loved me unconditionally.

To my family and the love of my life, who constantly encourage and influence me.

To Kahaleh & Lebanon, the land that nurtured my dreams and inspired my vision.

To the land of opportunities, the USA, whose corporations have opened endless possibilities for me.

And to Canada, my second home, a country that welcomed me with open arms and provided new beginnings filled with hope and promise

ACKNOWLEDGEMENTS

Writing this book has been a journey, one that could not have been completed without the support, patience, and love of many individuals.

Firstly, I would like to express my deepest gratitude to my late father and mother. Their unwavering belief in my capabilities has been my anchor, and their wisdom is my guiding light. My late father, with his exceptional leadership, resilience, and unyielding spirit; and my mother, with her grace and nurturing love; have always been my most profound sources of inspiration. This book is as much theirs as it is mine.

I would also like to express my deep gratitude to my family, particularly to my wife and four children. They have always stood by me through the highs and lows of this journey. Their support and encouragement have been the backbone of this endeavour.

I extend my heartfelt appreciation to my past and current mentors, whose knowledge, guidance, and patience have been instrumental in my life. Their insightful critiques and untiring support have shaped the course of my life and had direct input into this work.

I am immensely grateful to my publisher, whose professionalism and motivation drove this book to its present form. Their dedication to this project has been truly commendable. My sincere thanks go to my editorial team, who worked relentlessly to polish this manuscript. Particularly to Angie, Clare, Shobha, Mike, Emile and Carelle, their meticulous attention to detail and unwavering commitment have helped hone this work to its finest form, not to forget their tolerance and patience while pushing on my continuously moving deadlines.

To my friends and my colleagues at Infomed, who provided me with an unfailing support system, your constant encouragement and faith in me played a crucial role throughout the course of this project.

I am deeply indebted to the inspiring love that illuminates my path forward and the unlimited faith in my abilities; these did not just shape this book but also changed the course of my journey. The presence of this immense love in my heart has coloured every word of this work, infusing it with a passion that words can barely express. This achievement is a testament to this powerful influence.

Finally, to you, the reader, who lends this book its true value and purpose, thank you for embarking on this journey with me. Without you, this book would be incomplete.

INTRODUCTION

Charting the Uncharted Path

Navigating the Intricacies of Choices and Behaviours

In the vast tapestry of life, every thread tells a tale, and every weave crafts a lesson. As we step into the ever-changing world of professional and personal pursuits, we find ourselves constantly tugged between decisions and dilemmas, priorities and passions. The dance between these elements isn't merely about achieving success: it's about understanding oneself, recognising what truly matters, and cultivating behaviours that reflect our innermost values and desires.

Consider, for a moment, the multitudes of choices we encounter each day. Priorities, often seen as mere points on a to-do list, are in fact our silent compasses. They shape our actions, guide our decisions, and more often than not, dictate the roads we tread upon. In the vast expanse of opportunities and challenges, how does one decide which path to take, especially in the dynamic landscapes of entrepreneurial endeavours or globalised frameworks? It's an intricate ballet, where one's internal metronome of values must be in sync with the external rhythm of circumstances.

Then, there's behaviour: a complex blend of learnt traits, inbuilt instincts, and conscious choices. In a world that's increasingly interconnected, our behaviours are more than just personal expressions; they are ripples that influence global currents. Whether it's understanding the subtleties of globalisation from a fresh perspective or acknowledging the profound power of affection in professional realms, our behaviours mould the essence of our journeys.

In the pages that follow, you will uncover diverse insights from strategies driven by deep-seated philosophies to the secret ingredient that propels success. But, more importantly, you will be invited to introspect. To ask difficult questions. To evaluate your priorities and to ponder upon the behaviours that truly resonate with your core.

So, dear reader, as you embark on this expedition, remember that every choice, every behaviour has the power to shape not just your destiny, but also the narrative of the world around you. Are you ready to navigate the intricate maze, to decipher the delicate balance of priorities, and to consciously craft your behaviours? Let this book be your guide, your mirror, and perhaps, your compass in the myriad pathways of life.

Balancing Acts: Leading with Adaptability and Heart

In the business world, consistency and change go hand-in-hand, even though this might seem counterintuitive. While maintaining a stable business often requires continuous adjustments to meet evolving challenges, achieving growth demands a relentless quest for new opportunities. In simpler terms, to keep a business steady, you have to be adaptable and ready for change. At the same time, if you want your business to grow, you cannot stay content with the status quo; you must actively seek out and explore new frontiers. So, even if it sounds contradictory, this balance between stability and exploration is essential for a business to thrive and expand. From this perspective, I encourage readers to sculpt their professional journeys, continuously seek new challenges, and venture beyond their comfort zones.

The discourses around leadership, strategy, career paths, people management, and strategic thinking have been abundant and ceaseless. These subjects have been the focus of top leaders globally. Despite my humble journey, I have taken the liberty to pen down my thoughts on these pivotal topics. Through my anecdotes and theories, I hope to offer you an alternative perspective in your quest to become the best version of yourself.

Some ideas presented, may invite debate or controversy, given the subjective nature of the topics, as they are driven by personal experience. Regardless, I want to emphasise the honesty and sincerity embedded in each analysis and explored topic.

While logic and theory form the foundation of each concept, there's room for emotions and heart in acknowledgement of our unique human conditions and specific circumstances. The content may not apply universally, but I encourage you to approach it from a different vantage point, to challenge yourself.

Approaching my ideas with an open mind and devoid of preconceptions about the past may assist you in developing your leadership style, enabling you to lead in a more transformational way, while staying true to yourself.

I would like to share with readers a perspective on leadership that has shaped my journey. You will meet a leader who values his team deeply, who acknowledges missteps and grows from them, who is not hesitant to offer apologies, and who seeks to understand colleagues at every level. In simple terms, I hope to offer insights that might guide you on your own path to becoming a more compassionate and effective leader, drawing inspiration from figures such as Steve Jobs.

Steve Jobs is a figure from whom I have drawn considerable insight. His achievements are nothing short of remarkable; he played an instrumental role in revolutionising the world. Yet, he was resolutely result-oriented, focusing on team outcomes irrespective of the immense compromise and sacrifice required from the team to attain their objectives.

Apple's unparalleled success under Jobs' leadership, driven by his visionary ambition, leadership style, and particularly his communication approach with his team, still prompts questions about his leadership style. I often ponder not just about his results, but also about what might have been different had his legacy included a more empathetic and supportive approach towards his team. Perhaps Apple might have achieved even greater heights if Jobs' leadership style had been different. This book aims to provide clarity on how you can chart your professional journey to increase the likelihood of success. While my theories may not be universally applicable to every circumstance or environment, they are grounded in the pragmatic lessons drawn from both failure and success. In instances of failure, I have learnt the value of avoiding repetition. While in the face of success, I have understood the significance of replication when feasible.

My modest hope is that, where ever you are in your career journey, some reflections in this book might resonate with you. Be it as a student, manager, or someone in a leadership role, I offer these principles with the wish that they will find relevance in their professional life, personal space, or broader societal interactions.

Join me in the upcoming chapter to uncover a narrative that begins on the war-torn streets of Lebanon, and reveals the transformative power of education. Within these pages, you will witness the evolution of a person, shaped by challenges but driven by an unwavering purpose. Together, we'll traverse a path laden with trials and invaluable lessons.

1

MY JOURNEY

From Lebanon's Battlefront to Business Frontiers

Leadership Lessons from a Tumultuous Journey

A purpose-driven message

My purpose in writing this book and sharing my journey is to offer insights drawn from my experiences and the valuable lessons they have imparted. I emphasise the significance of making informed choices and nurturing positive behavioural patterns. I have written this as a reference for those driven toward success but who might feel constrained by limited resources or direction. It is tailored for those manoeuvrings through the complexities of academia or grappling with diverse professional hurdles, all the while lacking the guidance of a seasoned mentor. Through this work, readers are welcomed to delve into leadership viewpoints rooted in practical experiences, with the hope of filling the mentorship gap and promoting confident, well-informed decisions.

The reality of life

My life began in a small town in Lebanon called Kahale, just ten minutes outside of Beirut. I, along with my two brothers and two sisters, were raised in a conservatively middle-class environment. We were brought up in a family that placed great value on education and a grounded moral compass. Our parents saw education, infused with a strong adherence to religious principles, as our path to a bright future. Along with my siblings, I was sent to a French Catholic missionary school, Freres de la Salle and I later studied Finance at St. Joseph University.

The backdrop of my upbringing was a tumultuous one, as my country was embroiled in a devastating war. Being brought up during the Lebanese conflict shaped my worldview significantly. My hometown, Kahale, was located on the battlefront, where severe clashes occurred regularly. The uncertainty and fear were palpable every day, with the trauma of losing friends and relatives. We were forced to evacuate our home several times due to the intensity of the battles.

Despite the relentless war, not once did we miss a day of school. I recall my father driving us to school in the early mornings, even after nights filled with the thunder of bombardment. He was resolute in his belief that we must not miss out on our education, that it was an investment in our future, a future that was shrouded in uncertainty and unpredictability.

The mid-1980s saw Lebanon grappling with a severe currency devaluation, with the Lebanese Pound losing more than 90 percent of its value. This economic crisis thrust us into a situation of limited resources, forcing us to downsize our standard of living. However, my parents never wavered on one thing: our education. They ensured we continued at our chosen institutions, believing in the power of education to transform our lives. Even though they themselves did not have the privilege of advanced education, they inherently understood and valued its transformative power.

Now, when I look back at my childhood and the harsh conditions it was fraught with, I choose to focus on the key learnings from what transpired:

- The war shaped my worldview, instilling me with resilience from a young age and helping me prioritise my choices and needs effectively.
- Moving from place to place honed my adaptability skills and enabled me to keep expanding my network.

- Having personally experienced the realities of war and its hardships, I've come to deeply understand compassion and the profound essence of empathy.

Uncertainties create opportunities

There are many people who have experienced difficulties in uncertain economies. They have worked hard to survive the politics of a country and the pressure to build a secure career path. Through the course of my own journey, I have faced such unknowns that led me on a path to transform my life.

Growing up in the volatile no man's land between two clashing factions in Lebanon, the daily realities of my existence revolved around the essential, and often hazardous, tasks of survival. To paint a clearer picture, there were zones so dangerous that setting foot in them was synonymous to inviting death, courtesy of hidden snipers. Decisions as routine as choosing a route were filled with life-altering implications. I recall times when, instead of charting out an academic day, I was strategising the safest paths to avoid sniper fire. My university itself was situated precariously close to the demarcation line; a single misstep or wrong turn could have been fatal.

In such an environment, the luxury of dreaming and fostering aspirations for a prosperous future felt remote. The idea of plotting an educational and professional course wasn't just challenging; it often felt like a distant mirage amidst the immediate threats that loomed large every day.

Added to this, the hyperinflation crisis that rocked the mid-eighties and stripped my father of his life's savings, irreversibly impacted his financial stability. This setback cast a significant shadow over my educational pursuits. However, it failed to dampen my resolve to chase my ambitions and dreams relentlessly. My goal was to keep striving and find a way out of the crisis.

Finding solutions

Throughout my life, I have perpetually sought out fresh journeys, opportunities, wisdom, encounters, and experiences. This unquenchable thirst for discovery, ingrained in me since childhood, has propelled me to explore new territories and continually broaden my horizons.

Certainly, my journey has not been without its share of challenges, but my unwavering determination, resilience, and adaptability have allowed me to surmount most obstacles.

Constrained by the limited opportunities in Lebanon, I ventured beyond the comfort of my homeland at the age of twenty-three.

Apart from family gatherings, I haven't looked back since, immersing myself in the adventure of adapting to new cultures, people, professional environments, responsibilities, and challenges.

I have had the privilege of residing in numerous countries and assuming over fifteen distinct roles, traversing fields from finance to commerce, executive positions, and even board-level positions. Of course, there are always costs associated with taking such a path.

I would like to share a poignant memory that remains etched in my mind. During the war, when power outages were frequent, our house would get bitterly cold in the winter. To keep us warm, my mother would heat an iron in front of the chimney and then run it over each bed. One by one, she would call us to snuggle into the warmed sheets. Years later, when I moved to Kuwait, which is known as one of the warmest countries in the world, I found the bed chillingly cold. It was a stark contrast to those harsh winter days in Lebanon, where, despite the biting cold, my mother ensured our beds were always invitingly warm.

My comfort zone

Adopting a priority-centric mindset, dreaming big and believing in their potential to operate beyond their comfort zones, is the most effective way for individuals to overcome their greatest obstacle. Many fall into the trap of complacency, remaining within their comfort zones without challenging themselves or adjusting their priorities. They don't explore their potential, often adopting an attitude of 'Why bother?' The choice between remaining comfortable or continually pushing oneself is crucial.

Adapting to various cultures and environments presented me with numerous opportunities. Being born and raised in Lebanon, then moving to North America, Europe, and the Gulf region, broadened my horizons and I discovered my potential.

Let me provide you with some concrete examples in this regard.

Proficiency in multiple languages: Moving from Lebanon to various countries improved my proficiency in multiple languages, making me an ideal candidate for a role as a global ambassador in a multinational company, in which communicating across different regions is essential.

Understanding diverse business practices: Each region, the Middle East, the U.S., and Europe, has unique business practices. Adapting to these different environments has broadened my outlook on international business and made me versatile in dealing with diverse professional situations. My international experience has been a major asset in business negotiations with partners from different cultures. I understand the different negotiation styles and expectations, resulting in successful deals that benefit all parties.

Cultural adaptability: Experiencing various cultures firsthand has likely enhanced my sensitivity to cultural norms and expectations, which is invaluable in today's globalised world. When managing a diverse team at work, I am able to mediate misunderstandings between team members of different cultural backgrounds by leveraging my understanding of their cultural norms.

Expanded worldview: Living in multiple countries certainly broadens one's worldview. This has enhanced my problem-solving and creative thinking by enabling me to approach challenges from multiple perspectives. I usually propose innovative solutions to problems in my company's brainstorming session; most of these innovative solutions are inspired by practices I have observed while living in different places.

Personal growth: Living in different cultures has undoubtedly led to significant personal growth, helping me discover new aspects about myself and teaching me how to thrive in various environments. Leaving Lebanon at a young age made me self-reliant and adaptable. These qualities later helped me to take the initiative and successfully lead a critical project at work.

Networking: Each time I moved, I had the chance to build a new network of friends, colleagues, and professional contacts, providing various opportunities for personal and professional development. For instance, I was introduced to a leading professional in my field through a connexion I made while living in the Gulf region. This connexion later led to a job offer from a top company in my industry.

Sharing my Experience: A visionary leader in healthcare

My academic credentials comprise of an Advanced Management Programme degree from Harvard Business School and a Master's Degree in Finance from St. Joseph University. My expertise has been further honed through executive programs facilitated by my former employers and conducted by prestigious institutions, including INSEAD, the University of Barcelona, and Case Western University.

Throughout my international career, I have had the distinct privilege of working with top-tier companies, celebrated for their robust developmental programs. My journey includes stints with globally recognised organisations such as Arthur Anderson, Abbott Laboratories, and AbbVie. Holding senior roles with these firms has immensely enriched my professional trajectory, allowing me to work alongside esteemed leaders and premier consulting firms. Currently, I serve in advisory and strategic capacities, whether as a partner, board member, or lead advisor, for prominent regional multinational healthcare firms.

I have also held many voluntary positions; I am the incumbent Chairman of the Don Bosco Culture Centre, an organisation committed to enhancing individual capabilities and capacities. Additionally, I hold a board membership with Maison Du Futur, a think-tank organisation, and act as Co-Director of the Harvard Health Care Association in the Middle East Region.

Armed with a varied educational and professional journey, has tremendously enriched my insights on finance and business management. Occupying roles in commercial and general management has provided an avenue to view businesses from diverse perspectives. Leadership responsibilities cultivated an approach rooted in genuine regard for colleagues, an approach validated by feedback from various professional circles. One of the significant takeaways has been the ability to support and uplift colleagues, underscoring the continuous nature of learning and self-improvement.

Challenges, particularly from earlier phases of life, have been less about individual accomplishments and more about the universal values they have instilled: resilience, adaptability, and determination. When posed with questions about age and experience during an interview, the emphasis was on the depth and breadth of professional exposure rather than mere years. Collaborations with top-tier corporations and learnings from industry leaders have enriched this journey, covering different regions and sectors, not to mention the invaluable life lessons from challenging years in Lebanon.

2

SUCCESS IS A LIFE JOURNEY

Navigating the Dynamic Interplay of Skills & Behaviour for Sustainable Achievement & Fulfilment

Success as a Holistic Journey

Many people often contemplate the factors behind varying levels of success in their professional endeavours. It's important to realise that success is not solely determined by technical prowess but also deeply rooted in behaviour and decision-making skills. One common mistake is prioritising *what* needs to be done while neglecting *how* it should be executed.

For example, consider learning to play the piano. It is crucial first to master the technical aspects, like hitting the right notes and reading sheet music. At the same time, it is equally vital to infuse your performance with emotion and expression: the *how*.

Similarly, in your professional journey, technical skills are important, but how you apply them through effective communication, teamwork, and ethical decision-making is equally critical.

Personal Experience: A Lesson in Leadership

I once worked with a brilliant manager who excelled in technical expertise but lacked in acknowledging achievements or offering encouragement. His leadership style caused high turnover and discomfort among employees, ultimately leading to his departure. This experience underscores the importance of strong leadership that instils positive behaviours in a team.

In conclusion, 'The What' (technical knowledge) and 'The How' (behaviour) both play essential roles in achieving success, but they impact team satisfaction and the sustainability of success, differently. Integrating both aspects allows us to foster sustainable, positive, and successful outcomes.

The Role of Behaviour in Modern Success

In today's world, individuals are evaluated not only based on their skills, but also on their demeanour, ability to establish connections, and capacity to create rapport. Job interviews are about more than just academic or professional knowledge; they also involve the ability to present oneself with confidence. Our behaviours inevitably influence others' perceptions of us.

The Fundamental Question

So, what behavioural skills should we adopt, and what choices should we make to enhance our prospects for success?

Taking Responsibility for Our Own Success

Many competent employees fail to progress in their careers, often attributing their stagnation to external factors. However, we often overlook our potential contributions to these setbacks. In the journey of personal and professional development, introspection is the starting point. Engaging in self-analysis enables us to identify personal weaknesses and the internal transformations needed for progress. This perspective empowers us to turn failures into stepping stones towards growth and success.

Leadership and the Balance Between 'The What' and 'The How'

During my leadership in the Middle East and Africa region, I encountered a challenge where a small subset excelled in 'The What' but lacked in 'The How,' which drew an undue amount of attention away from the larger team that consistently delivered and fostered a positive work environment. Sustainable success is about harmonising technical skills with positive behaviours.

The New Marketing Lead

When we hired a marketing lead with impeccable credentials but poor collaborative skills, it led to missed deadlines and morale issues. Despite technical brilliance, the inability to collaborate effectively and value the team's input proved detrimental. This experience highlighted the importance of balancing 'The What' and 'The How' for team success.

The Importance of Effective Communication

During an annual business review, I had strong technical content but struggled with presentation skills and audience engagement. This experience emphasised the significance of not only knowing your material but also delivering it effectively.

Balancing 'The What' and 'The How'

In all these scenarios, a crucial lesson emerges: while technical skills form the foundation of our professional lives, how we apply them, interact with others, and adapt to situations is equally pivotal. Emphasising both 'The What' and 'The How' ensures a holistic approach to professional success.

I have included a nine-box evaluation grid as an illustrative tool commonly used in talent management and performance assessment. This grid is adapted from industry-standard practices and is provided for demonstrative purposes of the balancing factor of The "what and How".

High Behavior	5 Low Performer High Behaviour (Warning - or change function)	2 Medium Performer High Behaviour (Potential)	1 High Performer High Behaviour (High Potential 2%-5%)
Medium Behavior	6 Medium Behaviour Low performer (Potential layoff)	4 Medium Performer Medium Behaviour (Well placed)	3 High Performer Medium Behaviour (Potential)
Low Behavior	7 Low Performer Low Behaviour (Potential layoff)	8 Medium Performer Low Behaviour (Potential layoff)	9 High Performer Low Behaviour (Warning - or change function)
	Low Performer	Medium Performer	High Performer

Identifying the Missing Element

Many individuals recognise career challenges only in hindsight and react to setbacks rather than proactively preventing them. In many organisations, only a small fraction of the workforce is considered 'high potential,' leaving the majority with ambiguous career paths. The crucial element missing from their mindset is often the correct prioritisation and productive behaviours.

Prioritisation and Behaviour

Establishing genuine priorities is an art that requires introspection and discipline. Focusing on too many tasks without clear priorities can lead to burnout and subpar work. Misguided behaviours, such as prioritising personal success over collaboration, can hinder long-term success.

Ambitions Aligned with Capabilities

Many individuals have ambitions that surpass their current capabilities. Aligning our capabilities with our ambitions is key to achieving our goals. The Future Success Equation helps us assess this balance and make necessary adjustments. If our ambition exceeds our capacity, it's a call to develop new skills. When capacity surpasses ambition, it's time to seek new challenges or leadership positions.

Future Success Equation:

Future = (Capacity) 'What I can do' / (Ambition) 'What I want to do'

$$Future = \frac{What\ I\ can\ do}{What\ I\ want\ to\ do}$$

Source: The equation is inspired by Arthur Brooks' concept of *From Strength to Strength*, emphasising the significance of aligning your ambitions with your existing capabilities for personal and professional success.

In this equation, *Future* represents your potential for success, and it's determined by the relationship between *Capacity* and *Ambition*.

Capacity (What I can do): This is the numerator in the equation. It stands for your current abilities, skills, knowledge, and resources: the things you are capable of achieving based on your existing competencies. It's essentially your starting point, where you are right now in terms of your skills and abilities.

Ambition (What I want to do): This is the denominator in the equation. It represents your aspirations, goals, and what you aim to achieve in the future. It's where you want to be and what you hope to accomplish.

Now, let's look at how this equation works:

When Ambition Exceeds Capacity

If your 'Ambition' (denominator) is much larger than your 'Capacity' (numerator), it signifies that your goals and aspirations are more significant than what you can currently handle with your existing skills and resources. In this case, you might be aspiring for things beyond your current capabilities. It means your ambitions are high, but you're not fully prepared to reach them.

$$\text{Future} = \frac{\text{What I can do}}{\text{What I want to do}} < 1 \implies \text{Needs Development}$$

When Capacity Exceeds Ambition:

Conversely, if your 'Capacity' (nominator) significantly surpasses your 'Ambition,' it means you are overqualified or underutilising your current skills and resources relative to your goals. Your capabilities exceed what your current objectives require. You might be capable of more than you're currently aiming for.

$$\text{Future} = \frac{\text{What I can do}}{\text{What I want to do}} > 1 \implies \text{Assume Higher Responsibility}$$

The equation encourages continuous self-assessment and alignment. It emphasises that personal and professional development can help you adjust your ambitions to match your evolving capabilities. This way, your goals remain achievable and challenging, helping you progress toward success in your journey.

The Journey Ahead: Determining the Direction

In the next chapter we will explore various topics that illuminate the path to a more fulfilling professional and personal journey, from making the right choices to creating a guiding life philosophy. The aim is to equip you with insights and tools to balance your capacity and ambition for a successful future.

In any journey, the crucial step is deciding on the direction to take. This direction should be determined by three fundamental questions:

Where to go?

What is it for me?

How to get there?

Let's delve into these vital questions and work to elucidate the answers.

3

SETTING YOUR PRIORITIES

Paving the Way to Success

Many individuals from the developing world receive quality education and harbour big dreams. However, a gap exists due to the lack of proper orientation about the demands and potentials of the real world. Through this chapter, I aim to help bridge this gap, providing the essential orientation needed for a fulfilling professional journey.

Setting priorities can be likened to building with pillars. In the same way that pillars serve as a crucial foundation for construction, priorities lay the groundwork for success. In the previous chapter, I hinted at the concept of priorities in a general sense. However, we will dig deeper into the subject matter in this chapter, offering techniques that are applicable to various life stages.

I will systematically illustrate how to accurately prioritise your choices during your professional journey. By creating your own journey map, you will be able to recognise each stage and identify the central priority within each one.

From my corporate experience, I've distilled what I believe are the five key stages of professional life. These include

a) education,
b) the first professional experience,
c) career building,
d) becoming a professional,
e) transitioning into a seasoned expert in retirement.

Consider, for example, the educational life stage. It's comparable to laying the foundation of a building. You're accumulating knowledge and skills, but you also need to prioritise the areas of study that align best with your career aspirations. It's the pillar upon which your career will stand.

As you transition into your first professional experience, you're essentially building the first floor of your structure. This is the stage where you start applying the knowledge and skills acquired during your education. The priorities shift towards excelling in your role, learning from more experienced colleagues, and understanding the intricacies of the workplace.

Career-building is akin to adding more floors to your structure. Now, your priority is not just to excel in your role, but to take on more responsibilities, lead, and strategise.

Your priority at this stage revolves around making significant contributions to your field and establishing a strong professional reputation.

Becoming a professional is like constructing the top floors of your building.

Finally, transitioning into a seasoned expert in retirement is like adding the roof and the finishing touches to your building. The priority here shifts towards mentoring the next generation, sharing your wealth of experience, and potentially contributing to your field in novel ways.

Just as every individual has the right to success within a corporate environment, everyone has the potential to construct a towering building, metaphorically speaking. Having seen numerous ambitious people in various stages of their professional journey, I've gathered a wealth of insights that I wish I could share with the younger generation or even with my younger self.

Learning to prioritise will enable you to isolate the important and urgent decisions to be made. Prioritising requires clarity and the ability to determine the immediate value of what needs to be done.

Priority

I envision prioritisation as a tripod, standing firmly on three crucial pillars:

1. Tools: The equipment, resources, or skills you have at your disposal. These can range from tangible items like a computer or financial resources to intangible assets such as your education, experience, or connections.
2. Options: The array of choices available to you at any given moment. This can include different paths to reach your goal, various methods to solve a problem, or even alternatives in a decision-making process.
3. Goal: The ultimate objective or the end result you wish to achieve. This could be a career milestone, a personal ambition, or a project outcome.

Each pillar has its distinct role, but they intertwine and influence each other. For instance, your available tools might affect the options you consider viable. Conversely, the goal you're pursuing could dictate the tools you need.

Consider an architect designing a building. Their tools would encompass their design skills, software, knowledge of materials, etc. Their options would include different design concepts, material choices, or construction methods. The goal would be to create a functional, aesthetically pleasing, and sustainable building.

The architect must prioritise based on these three elements. They might choose a design concept (option) that best aligns with the desired building functionality (goal) and can be efficiently executed with the software they're proficient in (tool).

Similarly, in your personal or professional life, understanding this tripod of tools, options, and goals can significantly enhance your prioritisation skills, helping you make decisions that are more strategic, efficient, and goal-oriented.

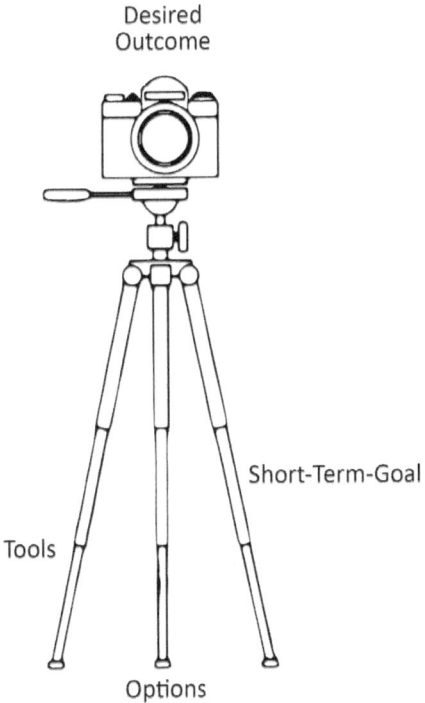

Tools Options Goals

The ideal blend of the three components: tools, options, and goals, should yield the optimal priority that will lead you towards your desired outcome. Let's clarify this concept with a straightforward example.

Imagine yourself as a 20-year-old student who has received an invitation to a dinner party. However, you also have a mid-term exam in two days that you're still preparing for, and you're under considerable stress to excel.

Your long-term desired outcome: To graduate with excellent grades.

How do you prioritise?

Analysing the situation:

1. Tools = Studying/Revision
2. Options = a) Attend the dinner party b) Stay at home to study
3. Goal = To perform well in the mid-term exam

In this scenario, studying is the tool that will help you achieve your short-term objective (doing well in your exam). The options presented need careful consideration to determine if they might impact your ability to utilise your tools effectively and jeopardise your short-term goal.

The process of such analytical thinking will help determine your priorities and guide you towards the successful accomplishment of your goals. If attending the dinner party compromises your short-term goal (doing well in the exam), then it's clear your priority should be to stay home and study since you're not yet fully prepared for the exam.

The long-term desired outcome, 'graduate with excellent grades,' is the sum of all these short-term goals. Therefore, it's crucial to consistently adopt this thought process to shape your decision-making pattern. By doing so, you'll be more likely to make choices aligned with your overall objectives, leading to success in your pursuits. As you discover and become adept at following these steps, they will become a part of your thinking as you go further in life.

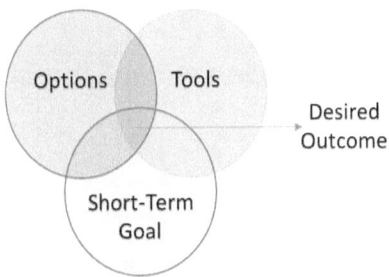

PROFESSIONAL STAGES

The progression of our professional lives is marked by distinctive stages, each with its own set of priorities and decision-making requirements. I have delineated these stages into five key phases that generally encompass one's professional journey:

Educational life: Education for money (University)

In this phase, you invest in education, the primary tool for shaping your future. Your choice revolves around the discipline or major you decide to pursue. Your goal is academic success. Here, the priority is intense studying to secure high grades and to enhance future prospects. Despite various distractions that university life might present, your focus should remain unwavering towards academic excellence.

First professional experience: Education for free (first job)

Fresh out of university, you are eager to embark on your first professional endeavour. Your 'tool' now becomes the nature of your first job, your 'choice' is the organisation you opt to join, and your 'goal' is to learn. Many fresh graduates fall into the pitfall of prioritising salary over learning opportunities in their first job, but remember, this phase is crucial for setting the groundwork for your career. Choose an organisation that holds a strong reputation and that provides rich learning experiences, irrespective of the financial returns.

Career building: Be known for one thing

By this stage, you should have a clear vision of your career path, whether it's in finance, healthcare, technology, or any other field. Your job is to consolidate your expertise in your chosen field, ideally within a well-known company that enhances your professional credibility. The financial return at this stage should be comfortable enough to support your family's needs. Choose a career that aligns with your passion and expertise.

Becoming a professional: Joining the C-suite

By now, you are a recognised expert in your field and are ready to transition into a leadership role at the executive level. You've become a reference point in your industry. While your employer's reputation still matters, it's not as important as it once was. Instead, ensuring a suitable financial income becomes more critical as you approach retirement.

Transitioning into a seasoned expert: The expert (The professional retiree)

This stage is all about giving back and leveraging your wealth of experience. As you retire from active service, you may consider joining boards or becoming a consultant, thereby imparting the knowledge you've amassed over your career. This is a time of less pressure, more teaching, and enjoying a different perspective on the industry you've spent your life in.

The diagram below encapsulates the professional journey by outlining the stages, objectives, and priorities. The key takeaway is to remember that each stage demands its own unique set of priorities, and understanding these can guide you to make the right choices at the right time.

SETTING YOUR PRIORITIES 37

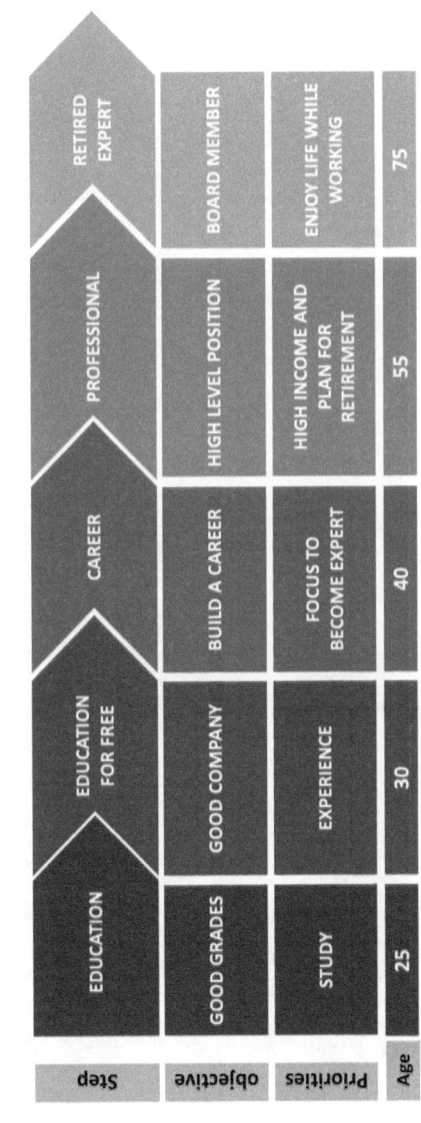

THE MAGIC RECIPEE BEHIND A PROFESSIONAL SUCCESSFUL JOURNEY

Properly Identify you objectives and your priorities at every step of your life

Step	Education	Education for free	Career	Professional	Retired expert
Objective	• Graduated from a reputable university. • Achieved good grades. • Specialized in a reputable field of study.	• Join a reputable company that offers educational opportunities and general experience. • Start at an entry-level position.	• Build a long-term career. • Progress to middle management.	• Become a professional and master the job. • Aspire to reach the C-suite (executive leadership) level.	• Serve as a board member. • Pursue a career as a freelancer.
Priorities	• Study • Learn • Network or Build Connections • Develop both hard and soft skills	• Seek a broad and valuable general experience from a reputable company to enhance my knowledge and prepare for the next career step. • Prioritize gaining expertise over high compensation.	• Learn a career and attain expertise in it. • Aim for a lifelong commitment to this career. • Currently in middle management, working towards a senior position. • Prioritize working in a reputable company. • Seek compensation sufficient to cover your expenses.	• Professional with extensive experience in your field • Earn respect for your knowledge and expertise • Part of the decision-making team • Actively developing your soft skills • Recognized as a reference within the organization • Financial responsibility, including saving, is a priority	• Self-sustenance as an independent individual • Desire to give back by supporting others in their success • Work for enjoyment or fulfillment • Financial stability • Ability to increase social responsibility • Consider education as an option
Age	25	30	40	55	75

The power of priorities

In developed nations, specifically the United States, individuals instinctively embark on professional journeys with the right mentality. This behaviour is largely influenced by a cultural backdrop that fosters competitiveness and a mindset of endless opportunities. The extensive economic landscape of the United States further amplifies these opportunities, enabling individuals to explore limitless possibilities.

However, in the Middle East, where regional and local enterprises play a more secondary role, I've observed many individuals becoming trapped in the system, unable to expand their horizons without external aid. In other words, they find it challenging to seize better opportunities or roles. These individuals could have made more strategic decisions early in their careers and acknowledged the repercussions of those initial choices. The issue lies in the fact that successful progression from one stage to another is only possible if the criteria of the previous stage have been appropriately fulfilled. For example, if you joined a company where learning opportunities were minimal during the 'education for free' phase, building a career and moving to the next stage would prove exceedingly difficult, if not impossible.

My intention behind outlining the five professional stages is to emphasise the importance of comprehending each phase of your professional life and making astute decisions accordingly.

While my choices weren't necessarily planned or advised, I was fortunate to move appropriately from one stage to the next. Upon graduating with decent grades in Accounting & Finance, I joined Arthur Andersen, a renowned company that offered three major benefits:

1. Exposure to multiple industries
2. A deep understanding of financial reporting, and
3. Proficient presentation skills, which I also like to call 'selling skills' – the ability to sell yourself, your ideas, your project, etc.

Let's explore and evaluate the professional status of some individuals, taking into consideration their age and ambition. When opportunities arose in my network, I noticed a consistent mismatch: either the age or qualification of the individual was not suitable.

When a professional opening emerges, you need to possess a balance between age and qualification to turn it into a winning opportunity. The absence of this balance makes it almost impossible to achieve your goal. I've encountered this situation multiple times, where people approached opportunities without a complete understanding of the requirements, lacking one of the other crucial elements.

For instance, when Carlos, currently product manager, aspired to the regional marketing position at the Immunity Division, his experience was adequate, but human resources expressed concerns about his age. In this case, they considered him either overqualified or lacking the energy required for the regional position's responsibilities. While age isn't a definitive factor in assuming new responsibilities, it remains an element that requires thoughtful consideration. Different age groups bring their own sets of experiences and perspectives, and it's essential to weigh these when evaluating suitability for certain roles or tasks.

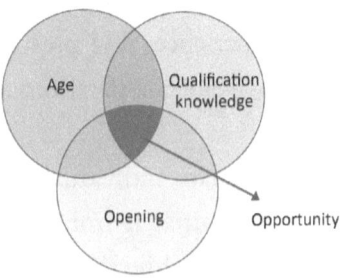

Qualification is a comprehensive construct encompassing three core components:

1. Technical proficiency: This refers to the specialised knowledge and skill set pertinent to your field or industry. It comprises your educational background, certifications, professional training, and practical understanding of the technical aspects related to your role. For example, a software engineer must be proficient in coding languages, data structures, algorithms, and software design.
2. Leadership acumen: This involves not only your ability to manage and motivate a team but also to make sound decisions, exhibit strategic thinking, demonstrate resilience in the face of challenges, and adapt to change. A great leader

effectively navigates complex situations, inspires others, and fosters a conducive work environment that promotes collaboration and innovation.
3. Credibility of source: This refers to the reputation and standing of the institutions or organisations where you've garnered your qualifications. It can be the university where you received your degree or the companies where you gained your professional experience. The prestige of these entities often influences how your qualifications are perceived.

For instance, consider two individuals, both possessing an MBA degree. One acquired it from a globally recognised institution like Harvard, while the other was from a lesser-known local university. Despite having the same qualification, the one from Harvard is likely to be perceived as more qualified due to the reputation of the institution.

The hurdle many people face is that while they might excel in technical knowledge and leadership skills, their qualifications may not be recognised or valued if acquired from less reputable or recognised sources. Consequently, this may result in missed opportunities, as the credibility of the source plays a significant role in the perception of an individual's qualifications.

Therefore, enhancing your qualifications requires you to focus not just on accumulating knowledge and developing skills, but also on choosing reputable institutions or companies for your education and professional experience. So, the issue of the credibility of the source is a valid concern that many individuals face when it comes to education and professional qualifications. As mentioned in the example, the reputation of the institution or organisation from which one obtains their qualifications can significantly impact how those qualifications are perceived by others.

However, it's essential to note that while attending a prestigious institution can certainly open doors and provide networking opportunities, it does not define a person's abilities or potential for success. Here are some strategies to help you if you didn't get your credentials from a reputable source:

1. Highlight skills and achievements: Instead of solely focusing on the name of the institution, emphasise your skills, achievements, and practical experiences. Showcase your expertise through projects, certifications, and real-world accomplishments.
2. Networking and building connections: Make an effort to network with professionals in your field. Building meaningful connections and gaining endorsements from respected individuals can help counterbalance the lack of a prestigious credential.
3. Build a strong portfolio: Create a portfolio that showcases your work, accomplishments, and expertise. This can be a powerful way to demonstrate your abilities and prove your worth to potential employers or clients.
4. Obtain certifications & demonstrate continuous Learning: Pursue industry-specific certifications or professional qualifications that are recognised and respected in your field. These can enhance your credibility and show a commitment

to continuous learning. Show that you are committed to learning and improvement by attending workshops, seminars, or online courses related to your field. This demonstrates a proactive approach to self-improvement.
5. Seek recommendations: Request recommendations from mentors, supervisors, or other professionals who can vouch for your skills and work ethic. Positive testimonials can carry a lot of weight.
6. Be confident and persistent: Confidence in your abilities and persistence in pursuing opportunities can go a long way in overcoming any biases related to the source of your qualifications.

Remember that while a prestigious institution can open doors, it is not the only factor that determines success. Many individuals have succeeded in their careers and made significant contributions to their fields without attending renowned universities or organisations. Ultimately, it's your skills, determination, and passion that will set you apart and make you stand out in your chosen field.

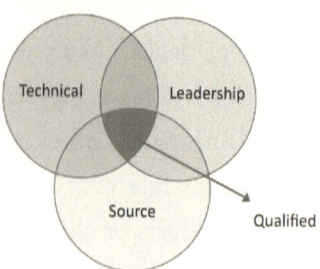

Relationship between the position and training types: blend between technical, leadership and source of the institution

When you begin your career, technical skills play a pivotal role. These are the specialised abilities and knowledge related to your field of expertise. Mastering these technical skills is essential for performing your job effectively and contributing to the success of the organisation.

As you gain experience and demonstrate proficiency in your technical role, you may be presented with opportunities for career advancement. Moving up the career ladder often means taking on leadership positions or managerial roles. At this stage, leadership skills become paramount.

Leadership skills encompass a wide range of attributes, such as communication, decision-making, problem-solving, delegation, and team management. These skills are vital for guiding and inspiring others, fostering a collaborative work environment, and achieving organisational objectives.

It's important to recognise that your career progression is not solely determined by accumulating years of experience. Instead, it's about developing a well-rounded skill set that includes both technical and leadership capabilities. Emphasising leadership skills as you advance in your career will enable you to effectively manage teams, drive innovation, and adapt to the challenges of leadership roles.

Ultimately, a successful and fulfilling career journey requires a balanced approach where technical expertise lay the foundation and leadership skills pave the way to new heights of professional achievement.

As illustrated in the diagram below, the progression of your career demands a shift in focus from technical skills to leadership skills as you take on increasing responsibilities.

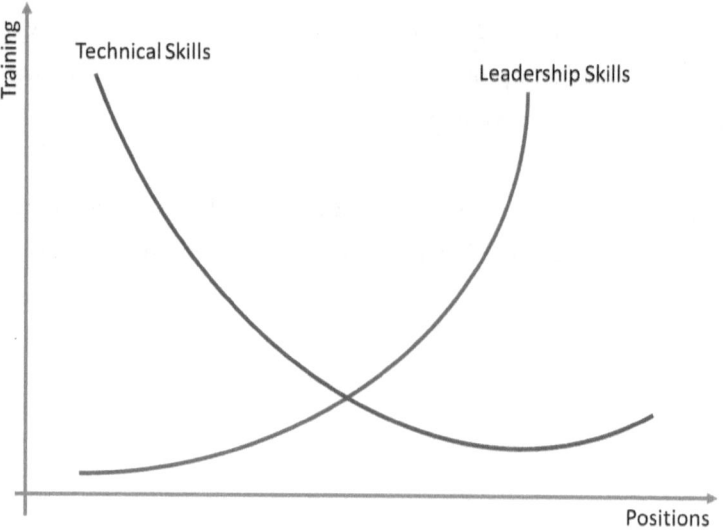

Summary

Essential factors: Are they universally relevant? Do they apply to all individuals?

The principles I've outlined relating to the five stages of your professional life a) educational life, b) the first professional experience, c) career building, d) becoming a professional, and finally, e) transitioning into a seasoned expert in retirement, aren't universal decrees. Like all things in life, various factors can delay or completely alter your trajectory. Yet, you can still achieve success and your goals, irrespective of the path you choose. These stages are particularly applicable for those embarking on a standard professional journey.

Consider the story of David, an aspiring entrepreneur, who jumped straight from the 'education for money' stage to 'becoming a professional.' David had a unique, innovative idea during his college years, which he turned into a successful business venture that bypassed several conventional stages. Here, his circumstances and the nature of his industry allowed him to merge multiple stages.

On the other hand, Samantha, who started as a junior analyst in a large corporate firm, adhered more closely to the outlined stages. She gained the necessary technical skills and gradually developed leadership skills as she ascended the corporate ladder.

Samantha's journey epitomises the conventional path that these stages represent.

In conclusion

By now, you're familiar with the five stages of a professional career. Reflect on these stages within the context of your own life. Perhaps you are like Lisa, a mid-level manager trying to break into the executive level. You might realise that you need to focus more on honing your leadership skills to reach the 'becoming a professional' stage. Don't give up on your dreams or priorities easily.

Discovering magic

This brings me to an essential concept: discovering the magic in your life. Consider the case of a CEO who transformed his company culture by encouraging innovation and creativity. In other words, he created 'magic.' Follow me in the next chapter as we uncover together the magic I encountered during my journey.

4

FIND YOUR MAGIC ROAD

We all need a Bit of Magic

Have you ever felt a spark, an inexplicable force, or a touch of enchantment in your life that elevates the mundane? It's this often-underappreciated element of magic that infuses our daily routines with vitality and propels us towards success.

Conducting business in a conventional manner will only get you so far. To truly unlock your potential and bolster your competitive edge, you need to infuse a dash of magic into the mix. I've felt this extraordinary magic in numerous significant milestones of my life, both personal and professional. For instance, the birth of my first son was a momentous occasion laden with intense emotion, a magical experience of witnessing the miracle of life.

People often assume that magic is uncommon, that it requires magicians to bring it to life. However, in this chapter, I want to underscore that creating magic is a part of our existence. It's ingrained in our human nature. Without magic, we cannot thrive, and as a leader, you indeed need to be a magician: weaving something extraordinary in your spirit, heart, and mind.

Magic permeates everything we do. It's everywhere; it's embedded in life if we're open to perceiving it. Let's say you're visiting a new city, and you unexpectedly stumble upon a unique musical rhythm of the locale. Even though the lyrics remain unfamiliar, you're delighted by the melody. This discovery might be small, but it sparks joy as if you've unearthed something special. That's magic.

There are moments when you forge connections with people in the most unexpected ways. Despite not knowing why, you realise you share a similar thought process and can almost predict each other's thoughts. That's magic.

How many times during a job interview have you felt an inexplicable connection with the person sitting across from you within the first fifteen minutes? That sudden sense of chemistry, that instant connection: it's magical.

In your professional journey, you must have relished that extraordinary sense of achievement and satisfaction upon closing a significant deal, earning a promotion, or convincing someone with a compelling idea. All of that encapsulates the essence of magic.

Magic is omnipresent. It surrounds us, floating around, waiting for us to tap into it, whether it's in our personal lives or professional endeavours. In this chapter, I'll share a poignant story of how a company driver transformed into a role model for all employees, manifesting how magic can be conjured from the most unlikely sources. I hope that by the end of this chapter, the magician in your heart will be awakened and that you will allow magic to permeate among all your team members.

Defining the characteristics of a magician

We all need to experience and embody the power of magic. This becomes possible when we foster a culture of creativity and innovation in our organisations.

During one of my workshops, we discussed the traits of a magician. Here are some of the responses:

- Smart
- Charismatic
- Perfectionist
- Captivating
- Can transport audiences to another realm
- Has the ability to make others believe in their ideas
- Inspires people
- Leads by example

- Executes plans meticulously
- Minimises mistakes
- Dreamer
- Innovator, Etc.

If we were to take the above and put it in the professional context and ask about the characteristics of a good leader, we'd receive strikingly similar responses. I believe that a potent leader is a magician: someone who possesses a vision for the future while being highly aware of changing trends. Authentic leaders have the power to influence and transform their teams in alignment with their vision, motivating and encouraging them to excel.

In our current digital era, knowledge is at our fingertips. Thanks to the rise of the internet and technological advancements, anyone can access almost any piece of information they want anytime, anywhere. This democratisation of information has led to a significant increase in educational attainment worldwide, resulting in more and more people achieving higher levels of education. The result is an incredibly competitive landscape where individuals must constantly strive to stand out from their peers.

Differentiating oneself in such a competitive environment is not solely about mastering technical skills anymore. Technical skills, while important, are becoming more common, as people have more opportunities to learn and develop them. Most technical skills, from coding to project management, can be learnt online through various courses and tutorials.

To truly distinguish yourself in today's saturated market, you need to go beyond technical competence. You need to have something unique, something that sets you apart. This is where the concept of 'magical allure' comes into play.

Magical allure represents the intangible, exceptional qualities that set you apart from the crowd. It's the creativity you bring to problem-solving, the emotional intelligence you apply in teamwork, the innovative thinking you use to navigate complex situations, and the personal charisma that makes people want to follow your lead. It's about harnessing your unique strengths, passions, and perspectives and bringing them to bear on your work.

Magical allure could also refer to your ability to inspire others, your knack for storytelling, or your capacity to see the bigger picture when others get lost in the details. It's these qualities, not easily learnt from a book or an online course, that make you not just competent, but extraordinary.

Therefore, you must strike a balance between technical competence and magical allure to stand out. It's about being skilled and knowledgeable, but also being inspiring, creative, and unique. This combination is what will help you stand out and succeed in today's highly competitive, knowledge-driven world.

a: Ambition and b: Innovation

Proper ambition paves the way towards a new horizon, sparking the search for novel methods and unprecedented opportunities. This process necessitates an unconventional approach and the constant pursuit of the unusual. The exploration of alternatives manifests into a 'need,' a compelling force that drives innovation. Herein lies the conventional route to innovation: through ambition, you discover the path to innovation, and to truly innovate, you require an element of magic.

Ambition will help you innovate; to innovate, you need magic.

In contrast to the typical definition, I view magic within the scope of this narrative as a series of events culminating in a desired outcome. For instance, consider a product launch. The process initiates with:

1. Market research to identify unmet needs
2. Assessment of the market size
3. Identification of potential opportunities
4. Development of a product positioning strategy
5. Creation of a product aligning with the above criteria
6. Preparation of the business model and infrastructure for product launch (warehousing, shipments, shelf space, etc.)

7. Training of the team
8. Launch of the product
9. Monitoring of performance

The aforementioned steps, encompassing the ideation/ambition stage to the product launch, should be perfectly synchronised and executed to reach a successful conclusion, creating what we perceive as magic. Magic, in this context, isn't merely a singular moment or isolated action. It's a cumulative sequence of events, each contributing to the realisation of a goal and culminating in a successful outcome. To elaborate further, we might define this 'magic' as a series of purposeful and transformative steps, each possessing its own touch of enchantment.

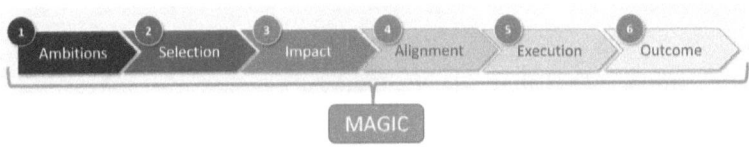

To create magic, one must thoughtfully design these series of events coherently (refer to the magic graph), utilising a holistic approach. Regrettably, magic doesn't simply occur when results meet expectations; it truly materialises when results exceed expectations. To elaborate further, imagine the example of a product launch.

Consider a technology company planning to launch a new smartphone. Meeting expectations might mean launching the product on time, ensuring it functions properly, and advertising it well. But to create magic, the company could go a step further. They might surprise their audience by unveiling an unprecedented feature, like an ultra-high-resolution camera that allows users to capture professional-grade images. The company could also engage potential customers by organising interactive, virtual launch events, turning the launch into an experience rather than just an announcement. Such initiatives not just meet, but exceed expectations, thus creating a sense of magic for the consumer /audience.

Below is a small definition of the illustrated graph:

1. Ambition: Represents the idea designed to address unmet customer needs.
2. Selection: Choose a concept that incorporates the most competitive differentiating elements.
3. Impact: Analyse both external and internal impacts from all perspectives, financial and non-financial.
4. Alignment: Ensure your infrastructure is prepared to accommodate the new concept and align with the desired outcome.
5. Execution: Ready your organisation for a proper launch and execution, ensuring 100 per cent implementation.
6. Outcome: Measure the outcome and compare it with the desired result. Revisit the steps above in case of variance in outcomes, either positive or negative.

Applied correctly, these steps combine with the desired results to create the remarkable magic of life. Look around and see how much magic you've woven thus far. When you count the moments, you'll realise just how many there are.

I'd like to stress that sometimes, due to circumstances beyond our control, we might not achieve the desired outcome. However, as long as we've taken all the necessary steps, I firmly believe we've still created something magical.

The Magical Directions

Allow me to share a personal event that has left an indelible mark on my life's journey. During my tenure at Abbott Laboratories, the company ushered in a fresh set of values: Pioneering, Achieving, Caring, and Enduring. After this announcement, every employee embarked on a journey of learning and internalising these principles through dedicated training and workshops. The aim was to ensure that each individual not only memorised these values but also deeply understood their true meaning and applicability in their day-to-day professional lives.

A visit from the company President to the Middle East was planned, during which we allocated a significant time slot for employees to share their testimonials about the company's values. The original idea was for the General Manager (myself) and all my direct reports to illustrate these values using real-life examples and personal perspectives. While this was an excellent opportunity to display a deep understanding of the values, I couldn't shake off the feeling that not all employees resonated with this approach. I considered including people from various organisational levels to share their experiences and interpretations.

This proposal garnered substantial interest, particularly because it provided an opportunity for wider exposure to the President. As we rehearsed and listened to these testimonials, I found myself content but not necessarily impressed, for they seemed nothing beyond the ordinary.

One day, as I was on my way to the airport, our company driver overheard my conversation with our Marketing Director about the quality of these testimonials. After I hung up, he humbly offered a different perspective in his modest command of English. He said, 'Sir, values are not just for managers and directors; values are for all employees. Let me share my story. When I am tasked with a myriad of errands like going to the bank, depositing checks, visiting the embassy, picking up couriers from the post office, and accomplishing all these before noon, it presents a challenge. But when I manage to do all this and return to the office before twelve O'clock, I feel a sense of achievement. But more than that, I feel like I am pioneering because I found a "Magic Road" in Dubai that helped me beat the heavy traffic.' He then added, 'Without magic, I cannot truly live the company values.'

His words served as a wake-up call. It was the answer to my concerns regarding the testimonials, and it presented an employee who could genuinely represent our branch in living the company values. This was my 'magic.' I immediately assigned someone to prepare our driver to present his testimonial to the President.

During the presentation ceremony with all our employees, the President and his staff in attendance, Tafasi was overwhelmed and humbly requested not to present. I stepped up to read his speech on his behalf, with him standing beside me. The response to this testimonial exceeded everyone's expectations. The President was profoundly moved and Tafasi was tearful. The President highlighted the importance of magic in our lives and encouraged each person to discover their own 'magic road,' just like Tafasi had.

Following the meeting, the President took Tafasi's recorded speech for the Board members to hear. Tafasi was later invited to be a guest speaker at our annual meeting, and his picture was posted on the company website as 'The Man of the Magic Road.' From that evening, the 'Magic Road' became our motto for two consecutive years, and we crafted our strategy and developed a set of behavioural skills around it.

During one of the annual meetings of the Middle East team, I embarked on a journey to Zimbabwe, specifically the Victoria Falls area, with the intention of seeking inspiration from the breathtaking beauty of nature and the magical African wildlife.

Despite the inconvenience of indirect flights, no one among the team complained, as the excitement of the expected experience filled us with an eager sense of adventure. The theme of the meeting was named 'The Magic Road,' inspired by the heartwarming story of our company driver.

After reaching Victoria Falls and completing our business reviews, we eagerly prepared for the game drive, anticipating encounters with magnificent animals in their natural habitat. However, we soon realised that the wet season had resulted in tall grass, limiting visibility and causing the animals to be less active.

As we drove around for hours without spotting any elephants, a sense of disappointment began to set in. The driver finally made the difficult decision to leave the reserve and head back to our hotel. I couldn't help but feel embarrassed and disheartened; we had come all this way to experience the magic of crossing paths with Africa's wild creatures, and it seemed like our expectations were not going to be met.

However, I couldn't give up that easily. I insisted that we spend more time in the reserve, hoping that our persistence would lead us to encounter one of these magnificent animals. Our convoy, consisting of around twenty cars, shared in the disappointment, but I believed there was still a chance for magic to happen.

And then it did. Just a few steps before we reached the main road, the driver in the leading Jeep suddenly came to a halt, his eyes fixed on a giant elephant standing majestically in the distance. As we watched in awe, we realised that a massive herd of over a hundred elephants was following behind.

A moment of sheer magic unfolded before our eyes: the herd of the magnificent elephants crossed the road, moving gracefully between our cars. For nearly half an hour, we were surrounded by these creatures, and time seemed to stand still. Words cannot describe the overwhelming emotions we felt at that moment: the joy, the awe, and the sense of being part of something truly extraordinary.

Some members of the team even shed tears, unable to believe the beauty of the coincidence that brought us face to face with these gentle giants. The magic of that encounter left an indelible mark on our hearts and minds.

I knew that I had found the core of my gala dinner opening speech: the story of Tafasi's magic road intertwined with our own magical experience in Africa. This encounter symbolised more than just a chance encounter with wildlife; it represented the power of determination, the refusal to give up, and the belief in our target and vision.

From that day onwards, 'The Magic Road' took on a whole new dimension for the team. It became a symbol of perseverance, reminding us never to abandon our dreams and to embrace the belief that magic can happen if we have the courage to pursue our ambitions with unwavering determination.

This magical encounter not only inspired us individually but also united the team under a common belief in the power of magic, both in nature and in our daily lives. The spirit of determination and the belief in the extraordinary continues to guide us in our pursuit of excellence and success.

The magic road in Africa taught us a valuable lesson: to see the world with wide-eyed wonder and to embrace the enchantment that life has to offer. It was a reminder that the most extraordinary experiences are sometimes born out of perseverance and unwavering faith in the journey ahead. It is a lesson that we carry with us, not only in our professional endeavours but also in our personal lives.

The magic road in Africa may have been a once-in-a-lifetime encounter, but its impact lingers on, reminding us that magic is not just an elusive force but a spirit that resides within us, urging us to reach for the extraordinary and embrace the beauty of life's most enchanting moments.

Cultivating magic: Key to success

Cultivating magic within your environment requires creating a supportive culture that allows for trial and error. This kind of culture fosters innovation by encouraging people to share their eccentric, ground-breaking ideas without the fear of failure. To conjure magic, you must be prepared to venture onto various paths, engage in diverse methods, and even set sail into unknown territories.

A prime example of this is when Christopher Columbus embarked on a voyage to discover a new world. Despite the uncertainty of the outcome, he dared to take the risk. The true magic of Columbus' journey wasn't in discovering America: it was the environment he fostered while planning the expedition, persuading the authorities, securing investors, recruiting a dedicated crew, and compelling society to adopt his vision.

Therefore, the foundational prerequisite for magic and creativity is the courage to try, without bearing the burden of guaranteeing success.

The Penguin Award

A fascinating survival strategy can be observed in the life of penguins. When the penguin colony is ready to dive into the ocean for a fish hunt, they risk being preyed upon by lurking seals and whales. In such scenarios, one brave penguin takes the plunge first while the rest of the colony waits and observes. Although this penguin might fail and become prey, its sacrifice ensures the survival of the colony.

Drawing a parallel to corporate environments, some organisations reward employees for such bravery, the willingness to fail in pursuit of innovation. These accolades, which I like to refer to as 'The Penguin Award,' are bestowed irrespective of the outcome. Without an environment that encourages risk-taking, innovation is stifled, and by extension, the spirit of magic is lost. 'Ref: Our Iceberg is Melting – John Kotter'

In summary

In essence, magic is not only about the moments or the end result, but also about the journey you embark, the risks you embrace, and the adrenaline that fuels your pursuit. Magic is the backbone of success and the lifeblood of creativity.

I started this chapter by outlining the characteristics of magicians and authentic leaders. Now, I want to conclude by identifying the elements that transform an ordinary leader into a magician. I emphasise two factors:

1. The ability to dream
2. The power to inspire others

Invitation to Reflect

Reflect on the instances in which you've conjured magic in your life. Consider the small victories, the persuasion of a stubborn person, an unexpected promotion, or outcomes that exceeded your expectations.

Magic isn't sheer luck, it is a process, a journey, a state of mind, a place, and an atmosphere. Magic is the culmination of all these extraordinary moments in your journey.

Having laid out this framework of magic, we will move on to the next chapter, where we will allow magic to influence our goals. We will explore how you can attain the best version of yourself.

5

REALISING THE BEST VERSION OF YOURSELF

A Guide to Personal Excellence

I frequently struggle with questions like: What is my best self or best version? How can I actualise it? How can I ensure I'm on the correct path towards becoming it? What are the fundamental pillars to construct my best version? Can I unlock my best self independently?

In this chapter, my goal is to elucidate the importance of these questions and how they shape each person's unique life journey. I aim to provide insights into the ingredients required to bring one's ideal self to fruition. Furthermore, I intend to bring to light the delicate balance between feeling irreplaceable while staying rooted in humility. Equipped with insights and real-world examples, this chapter promises to guide readers to introspect, evaluate, and streamline their journey to becoming the best versions of themselves.

We cannot ignore the crucial role of four key elements:

1. Motivation: the force that drives us towards our ambitions
2. Appreciation: the acknowledgement and validation of our progress, serves as a catalyst to manifesting our best selves
3. Development: development represents the active pursuit of knowledge, skills, and experiences that contribute to personal and professional growth. It involves setting learning objectives, acquiring new skills, and reflecting on our experiences to continually improve ourselves.
4. Reward: Lastly, reward plays a significant role in this journey. It's not just about external rewards such as promotions or raises, but also about the internal rewards. These include the satisfaction of achieving a goal, the happiness that comes from personal growth, or the fulfilment derived from making a positive impact.

In this journey of self-realisation, these four elements function together as the internal compass, guiding us towards the desired direction of our personal growth and excellence. Tom Peters, the renowned author of 'In Search for Excellence,' asserted that people reach their zenith of performance when they realise their best version. This raises an intriguing question: is our best self a destination, or is it a constant journey of evolution?

Motivation

Let's start by examining what motivation signifies for individuals and how it can be ignited. Motivation can be:

- A drive to excel
- A catalyst for ambition
- The necessary energy to take action
- The sustenance that keeps us moving forward

Without motivation, we lack the fuel required to power our engine of progress. How often have we noticed that when we are deeply engaged and motivated in a project, fatigue takes a back seat, and we find ourselves able to work tirelessly to see it to fruition?

As motivation surges, so does our energy. Generally, when we encounter a worn-out individual, it's likely that they are lacking motivation. If we wish to inspire people to exert more effort, the key is to foster motivation.

The paramount question then is, what kindles motivation in people?

- Recognition?
- Respect?
- Rewards?
- Appreciation?

- Experiences?
- Feedback?
- Content?
- Achievements?

Indeed, all these factors contribute to motivation. However, I will argue that people reach their pinnacle of motivation when they feel genuinely appreciated.

It's noteworthy that what drives motivation changes over time, influenced by factors such as age, education, and social status. Furthermore, motivation is time-sensitive; when given too late or too early, it loses its potency.

For instance, the motivational pull of a toy for a child is time-limited and age-specific. It works within a certain age bracket, but loses effectiveness as the child grows older unless the motivational tool is suitably altered. This vividly demonstrates how motivation must evolve to stay effective and meaningful.

Appreciation

Happiness = Appreciation = Efficiency.

Consider a parallel from everyday life: Why do we often pay more for a premium brand? It's because we perceive a greater value in the brand compared to others, both in terms of tangible quality and intangible brand reputation. Similarly, when a leader showcases appreciation towards a team member, it amplifies that member's intrinsic value, akin to a 'personal brand,' within the organisation.

The decision to express appreciation, much like the decision to buy, is based on perceived value. As leaders, when we appreciate, we're signalling that an individual's contribution exceeds the 'cost' of having them onboard. This cost doesn't refer solely to monetary compensation but includes time, resources, and the space they occupy in the organisational ecosystem.

When leaders actively acknowledge and appreciate the unique strengths, talents, and contributions of their team members, it does more than just boost morale. It instils a sense of purpose, fosters loyalty, and creates a conducive environment for innovation. It's this culture of appreciation that accelerates efficiency. People are more inclined to give their best when they feel valued.

Furthermore, for a leader, appreciation isn't just about acknowledging accomplishments. It's also about recognising potential, encouraging growth, and fostering an environment where everyone feels empowered to share ideas, take risks, and challenge the status quo.

Revisiting the crucial driver of motivation, which I believe is appreciation, it becomes evident that when people are appreciated, they perceive their worth and contribution as valuable. This relationship can be summarised in the equation:

Motivation = Appreciation = Value.

Consider this analogy. When we make a purchase, the decision is primarily based on the perceived value of the item in relation to its price. If the perceived value is less than the price, we opt not to buy. Conversely, when the value exceeds the price, we decide to purchase. This willingness to buy is intrinsically tied to the item's perceived value. It's a principle that holds true for many premium brands where people willingly pay higher prices because of the added value they perceive the brand offers.

Drawing a parallel to the professional realm, when I receive appreciation at work, it signifies that my value, or my 'brand', outweighs my individual cost. It indicates that my contributions are highly valued and that the output of my work is making a meaningful impact. To be appreciated means to be seen, to be acknowledged. It reinforces a sense of belonging on the team, underscoring the value that my presence and contributions bring to the table.

Appreciation = high value ⟹ Effective presence ⟹ Effective outcome

Let's analyse appreciation from the leader's perspective:

At the heart of an effective leadership strategy lies a profound understanding of appreciation. It's not merely about recognising effort; it's about validating the intrinsic value each individual brings to an organisation.

When seen through the lens of a leader, appreciation is a transformative tool that fosters an environment of happiness and efficiency,

To put it succinctly, a leader who appreciates is a leader who understands the intricacies of human potential. Such leaders not only magnify the strengths of their team but also create an organisational culture where everyone feels uniquely valued.

The ensuing section, 'I am unique,' delves deeper into the profound impact of this appreciation and its pivotal role in shaping an individual's sense of self within an organisation.

I am unique

Appreciation can foster a sense of irreplaceability, conveying the impression that one's role in the puzzle is utterly unique. Let's consider this from another angle. If I am appreciated, it implies I hold value. If this value can be readily replaced, it suggests I'm not unique.

As a leader, fostering a sense of uniqueness in each team member can inspire them to deliver beyond their potential. In the context of a family, each member is irreplaceable and unique. The dynamics in a work setting, however, may be slightly different.

One potential pitfall in a workplace is the risk of complacency. If I start to perceive myself as irreplaceable and unique, it may fuel my motivation, but it might also lead me to take things for granted and foster a false sense of indispensability. It's crucial to remember that, at the end of the day, we are all replaceable to some degree.

Feeling both unique and irreplaceable can be perilous if not handled with care and balanced properly. Both the giver and receiver of feedback must tread carefully; the giver should avoid overstating motivational feedback, and the receiver should avoid becoming overly complacent about their position. It's akin to a tightrope walk where maintaining balance is key. This balance is between feeling unique and irreplaceable and delivering quality outcomes. Bear in mind that the more you consistently improve your deliverables, the longer your sense of appreciation will endure.

When individuals feel appreciated and valued, it inherently cultivates a sense of responsibility to continuously elevate their performance. However, the leader and source of this appreciation needs to strike a delicate balance in motivating the team. When team members attain a sense of irreplaceability and appreciated value, it's essential to consistently remind them not to rest on their laurels but to remain engaged and continuously strive for improvement.

REALISING THE BEST VERSION OF YOURSELF

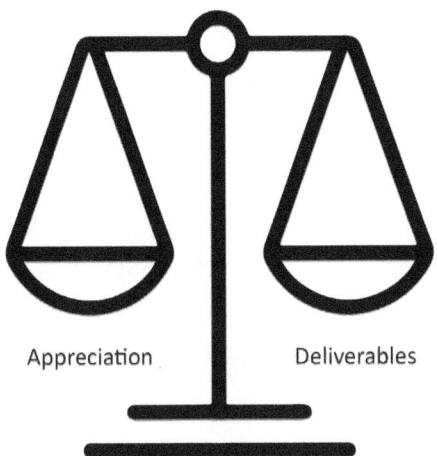

Appreciation — Deliverables

A perfect balance should be maintained between motivational feedback and Deliverables

Giver

Unique

Continuous improvement on deliverables

Receiver

Leaders' derailment

I learnt this principle at Harvard, and it perfectly fits into this concept. One common pitfall individuals often encounter is a gradual decline in their performance after they've achieved a certain level of success and appreciation. They ride the wave of past accomplishments, mistakenly thinking that these past triumphs will secure their future. However, the fuel of past success is finite and already expended. What truly matters is their present performance and preparedness for the future.

Numerous successful leaders have faltered on this account, falling victim to what is known as 'leader derailment.' Take dictators for example. When they reach a stage where they view themselves as uniquely untouchable and irreplaceable, they begin to take their position for granted, often acting erratically. Their opinions and judgments become unquestioned, invoking a sense of infallibility akin to the 'Papal Infallibility' concept (A doctrine in the Roman Catholic Church which holds that the Pope is incapable of error when he speaks on matters of faith and morals). However, this unchecked arrogance and disregard for continuous improvement ultimately leads to their downfall, sparking revolutions and their eventual defeat.

It's crucial to understand that the journey to success and self-improvement is continuous and ever-evolving. Resting on the laurels of past accomplishments can blind us to the need for continual growth, learning, and adaptation.

Continuous Improvement

Consider the case of loyal customers who leave us after years of patronage. This could be due to an oversight on our part, where we've perhaps taken their loyalty for granted. The principle of appreciation needs to be earned daily; it's a reciprocal cycle between the one who appreciates and the one who is appreciated. One party provides consistent motivation, and the other reciprocates with unwavering quality in their deliverables.

This cycle of appreciation should not be static but dynamic, keeping the appreciation environment alive and thriving. Breaking this cycle could lead to the disappearance of this appreciative atmosphere.

Therefore, it's of utmost importance to provide genuine feedback. When someone is appreciated, the recognition should be fair, honest, and credible. Be cautious, however, as excessive or undue appreciation can be detrimental.

The relationship can be clearly visualised on a graph. To prevent derailment and to maintain quality deliverables, continuous improvement and productivity must be pursued. The drive for excellence should be a constant endeavour, fuelled by balanced and credible appreciation.

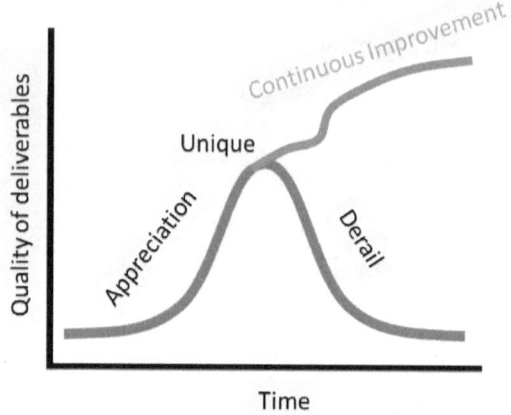

Financial reward and development driving potential

While financial rewards serve as significant motivators, their impact tends to be short-lived. Once individuals adjust to an increased income, the positive effect gradually diminishes. Although financial incentives are essential, particularly to retain top talent, they alone do not constitute a holistic approach to motivation.

On the other hand, motivation achieved through continuous personal and professional development is far more impactful and provides a better return on investment for both employees and the organisation. This type of motivation not only boosts the individual's skill set but also increases their value to the organisation, thus creating a mutually beneficial situation.

Thus, we arrive at the triad of motivation's essential pillars:

- Appreciation: Acknowledging an individual's contribution to the organisation instils a sense of worth and motivation to continue delivering quality work.
- Development: Continuous learning and professional growth keep employees engaged, challenged, and motivated, contributing to their job satisfaction and the value they bring to the organisation.
- Reward: Financial and non-financial incentives are vital in recognising hard work and fostering motivation, though they should be part of a larger motivational strategy.

For instance, consider Google's approach to employee motivation. The tech giant not only provides competitive salaries (Reward) but also fosters an environment of continuous learning and innovation (Development). It routinely recognises and appreciates its employees' efforts and achievements, often in team meetings or company-wide communications (Appreciation). This balanced approach to motivation contributes to Google's high employee satisfaction and low turnover rate.

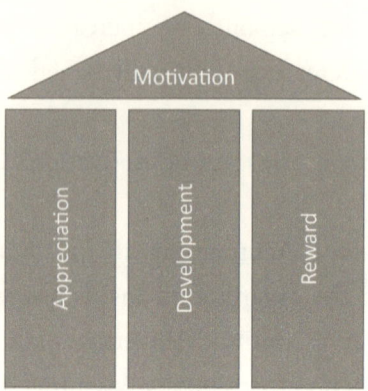

The three pillars of motivation

The triad of motivation and its evolution over time:

The prominence and impact of the three motivational pillars: development, appreciation, and reward, can vary, often depending on the progression and stage of your career.

Development

In the early stages of your career, for instance, as a recent graduate entering the workforce, development is typically the predominant pillar. You are in a phase of intense learning and skill acquisition, building a strong foundation for your future professional trajectory. As you progress and gain more experience, say as a mid-level manager, the need for such intensive development may taper off, although the quest for learning and adapting to new trends in your field should never completely halt.

Take the example of software engineers. Early in their career, they must focus on mastering programming languages, understanding algorithms, and learning about software architecture. However, as they progress and become project managers, they might need less hands-on development and instead focus more on management skills even though technical skills remain relevant.

Appreciation

On the other hand, appreciation remains consistently vital at every career stage. From junior employees to seasoned professionals, everyone desires acknowledgement for their efforts and contributions. Recognition fosters a sense of validation and can boost morale, engagement, and productivity. Just to say; appreciation should always remain at any stage of your career or age.

Rewards

The reward becomes increasingly crucial as you advance in your career and age. Commensurate compensation and rewards become a significant motivational factor as you climb the corporate ladder to positions with more responsibilities, such as a senior executive role. Additionally, as personal responsibilities, such as family or financial commitments, grow with age, the importance of rewards escalates accordingly.

For example, a senior executive might place more importance on equity-based compensation or retirement benefits than an entry-level employee who might focus more on the immediate salary or opportunities for skill development.

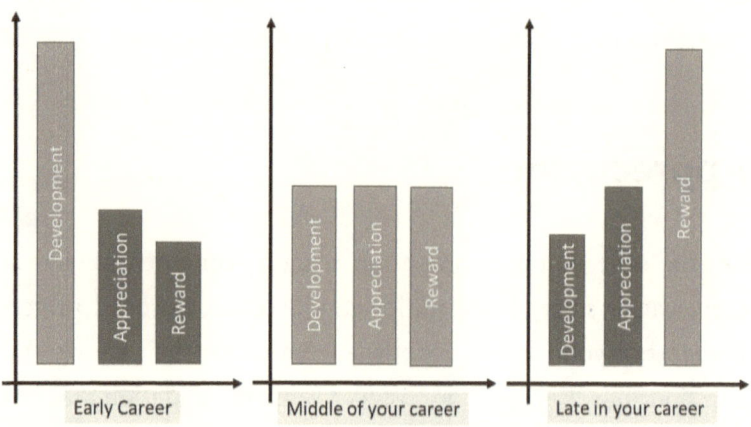

The inception of the 'best version' journey

The juncture where your needs for reward, appreciation, and development are sufficiently met heralds the onset of your 'best version' journey. Upon reaching this milestone, individuals often feel that they have truly embarked on their path to becoming their best selves.

That's why I prefer to regard the 'best version' not as a destination but as an ongoing journey. I like to refer to it as the pursuit of the 'best version.'

In the initial stages of your career or professional life, your focus is likely centred on honing your technical abilities and establishing your personal brand. Your self-confidence might still be in its nascent phase, and your primary goal might be to chart out the roadmap to guide you in the pursuit of your 'best version.'

As you progress in your career, everything begins to coalesce. Your value in your professional field escalates, your brand gains recognition, and your negotiation power strengthens. It's at this stage that the new era of the 'best version' begins to unfold. During this era, you transition into a position of influence, where your insights are highly valued, and your decisions carry weight. This evolution signifies the maturing of your 'best version' journey, setting the stage for continued growth and accomplishment.

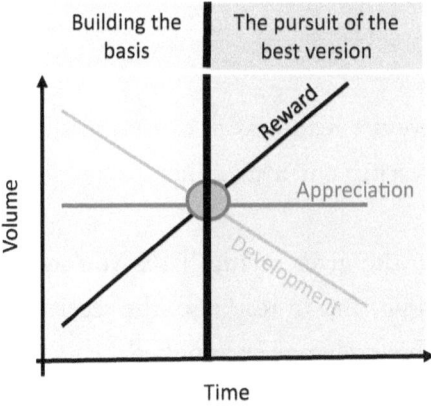

Attaining the 'Best Version' of self

As mentioned earlier, when the triad of motivation coalesce, an individual begins to perceive that they are on the path to realising their 'best version.' This confluence creates an environment conducive to retaining talent, as people are willing to offer their utmost and even make sacrifices within it.

In such a setting, individuals profoundly recognise the significance of their role in the larger scheme of things.

To illustrate this dynamic, let's turn to a unique tradition from Africa. When individuals from different tribes encounter each other, the first one greets the other by saying, 'I see you' (Giver or Initiator), to which the other (receiver) responds, 'I am here.'

'I see you' implies acknowledgement of the other's presence and their importance in the speaker's own understanding of humanity and objectives.

'I am here' conveys a readiness to assist and support, affirming the speaker's presence and availability.

In this context, the giver saying 'I see you' is acknowledging the receiver's value, and in response, the receiver affirms, 'I am here' for you. This exchange exemplifies the reciprocal nature of motivation.

In a positive work environment, this brief yet powerful dialogue can occur repeatedly, often without a single word being spoken. A smile at a co-worker signifies 'I see you,' a pat on the shoulder echoes 'I see you,' and a simple 'thank you' reaffirms 'I see you.'

Therefore, when you convey 'I see you' at work, be assured that the recipient is implicitly responding, 'I am here.' If you don't sense this response, it may indicate a lack of motivation on their part, suggesting that they are not fully present for you.

As previously discussed, motivation is a dialogue between several parties.

To draw another analogy, consider the nature of colours. Black is not considered a colour because it doesn't reflect light. We perceive colours when light is reflected back to us. Similarly, individuals lacking motivation are akin to the colour black, they don't respond or reflect back motivational actions. In contrast, a motivated individual reflects back the positive light of motivation, much like a vibrant colour.

Navigating the Motivational Dialogue: Initiating the Interaction

A pertinent question often arises; who should initiate this motivational dialogue? Who should be the first to express 'I see you,' prompting the response, 'I am here?' Determining who the initiator should be often creates a quandary.

However, if you truly value the process of motivation and strive to bring out the best version in each team member, the question of who initiates becomes less important. Regardless of your position or role, never miss an opportunity to show your team that you see them, and in return, affirm that you are present for them.

Let's take the example of a sports team coach. By praising a player for their effort during a game or training session ('I see you'), the coach fosters an environment where the player feels appreciated and is more likely to reply with even greater dedication and effort ('I am here'). This cycle can create a highly motivated and high-performing team.

Imagine a scenario on the same sports team where one player notices the extra hours another player is putting into practise. This observant player might approach their teammate and say, 'I've noticed how much extra time you've been investing. It's really pushing all of us to up our game. I see you.' The player who has been working hard, feeling recognised, might respond with, 'Thanks for noticing. It's all for the team. I'm here, giving it my all.'

Such interactions among team members foster mutual respect and camaraderie. It can strengthen the bond of the team and amplify the collective motivation. When teammates recognise and appreciate each other's efforts, it creates an environment where everyone feels valued not only by the leadership (in this case, the coach) but also by their peers. This peer recognition can be as potent, if not more so, as acknowledgement from the coach or leader. It highlights that every team member, irrespective of their role or stature in the team, has a part to play in motivating and uplifting one another.

Demonstrate your unique value to your team. If innovation is required, be the one to introduce fresh ideas. If hard work is needed, be the one to set the standard. Your team members will notice and appreciate your commitment, and they will reciprocate with support.

Personal growth in a global context: Striving for the best version of you

The pursuit of becoming the best version of oneself necessitates an unwavering commitment to personal growth and continuous learning. As you strive to unlock your full potential, you are empowered not only with heightened proficiency and expertise, but also with an enhanced capacity for influence and leadership. This transformation shapes you into an inspiring figure, a beacon of excellence to your peers, one they can look up to for guidance and inspiration. As you journey on this path of self-enhancement, you accrue a power that extends beyond your personal boundaries, enabling you to leave a permanent imprint on your environment and those around you. This journey, however, is not an isolated process. It takes place within a global context that is rapidly changing and intricately connected, which directly impacts you as an individual. In the subsequent chapter, we will further explore this intertwined relationship, delving deeper into the implications of globalisation and its direct and profound impact on your personal growth and pursuit of your best self.

6

THE POWER SHIFT

Looking at Globalisation from a Different Perspective

'You can now act globally. You can reach farther, faster, deeper, cheaper, in more ways and more days around more themes and subjects for less money than ever before as an individual. And that's what's new here.'

— Thomas L. Friedman, columnist, and author of *The World Is Flat: A Brief History of the Twenty-first Century*

This chapter is influenced by Thomas Friedman's book. However, the interpretation is different. I will explain it from two perspectives: individuals and enterprises.

I will also share with you the background of globalisation and how globalisation has affected people and companies from the shifting power definition.

I will start with a disclaimer: What you read in this chapter is not objective. It is purely reflecting my personal opinion; most of the content is cited by others.

The information you will read probably already exists in a corner of your mind. You may not have paid attention to it. All that I am doing here is to put it into sharp focus. I am shining the spotlight on this aspect of our globalised life and bringing this perspective to the forefront of your mind.

First, before you read further, take a piece of paper and write down what globalisation means to you. How do you define globalisation? And how do you feel it impacts you personally?

And also, I want you to think of globalisation as a power shift. So, when you write your definition, think of the power. Who controls the world?

Background

Let's take a step further back in time. To understand globalisation, we must look at some historical facts, how did it all start?

Globalisation has existed for ages. But it has been evolving and takes a different form based on the definition of the word and on the power holder. Every time the power moves from one entity to another, the globalisation effect takes on different meanings.

The Power shifts

Before 1490, the world was believed to be flat until Christopher Columbus had the courage to travel and sail across the world to disprove the theory. At that time in the fifteenth century, the global empire was not clearly defined. The global empire was not defined because humans thought they were at risk of falling off the edges of the earth when it was believed to be flat. But things changed dramatically when Columbus proved that the world was round.

This marked the beginning of the era of globalisation, as things began to evolve and take a distinct form. Before this period, the world was perceived as limited, with infinite resources. The understanding that the Earth is round implied that if one started from point A, they'd eventually return to that same point. Consequently, expansive empires, like the Roman Empire, evolved into a system of countries, kingdoms, or smaller entities governing their own territories. Before 1490, to have global relevance, one needed to be part of a dominant empire, such as the Roman Empire.

Between 1490 and 1800, following Columbus' realisation that the Earth was round, being global required association with one of the major kingdoms, such as England, France, the Netherlands, Portugal, or Spain. These powerful nations embarked on colonisation, expanding their territories extensively. Their might was often equated with robust teams of horses. Power was consolidated in the hands of a few and was measured by the number of horses owned, lands ruled, and territories occupied. This era gave rise to the concept of measuring power in terms of 'horsepower.'

Later, in the 18th century, the Industrial Revolution began, probably kickstarted by the discovery of the vapour machine. This launched a new era where the world began to get smaller. Technology was the reason behind this change.

Indeed, the shift from horsepower to machine power, which took place predominantly from the 1800s to the 2000s, marked a significant transformation in many aspects of society. This period witnessed the Industrial Revolution and subsequently the Technological Revolution, which led to a transition in power dynamics. Here are some prominent examples:

Standard Oil Company: Founded by John D. Rockefeller and associates in 1870, Standard Oil had monopolised the oil industry in the U.S. by the late 1800s. The company used its significant influence not only to shape the energy sector but also to manipulate political and legal environments to its advantage.

Carnegie Steel Company: Under the stewardship of Andrew Carnegie in the late 19th century, Carnegie Steel Company became a symbol of power and influence in the U.S. steel industry. This allowed Carnegie to have a significant impact on infrastructure and construction, as steel was a critical material in these sectors.

Ford Motor Company: Founded in 1903 by Henry Ford, the Ford Motor Company revolutionised the automobile industry with the introduction of the assembly line. This gave Ford a significant influence over not only the manufacturing process but also labour practices.

General Electric: Established in 1892, General Electric (GE) held considerable power in the electrical industry, producing a wide range of products, from light bulbs to industrial equipment. GE's influence extended to shaping public policy and standards for electrical goods.

Microsoft: Founded in 1975, Microsoft revolutionised the world of personal computing in the 20th century, wielding substantial power in the technology sector. The development of the Windows operating system placed Microsoft at the forefront of the technology industry and allowed it to influence global computing trends.

IBM: Established as a computing-Tabulating-Recording Company in 1911 and renamed IBM in 1924, it has wielded significant power over the technology sector for much of the 20th century. IBM's developments in computing, including punch-card technology, mainframe computers, and the invention of the hard disc drive, had a major impact on global business and technology.

These companies indeed held tremendous power, shaping industries and often swaying public policy. Their influence reached beyond their specific sectors, and impacted the global economy, technological innovation, and societal development.

Do you get the picture of how the power holder shifted with every changing period? Before 1490, the global empire was holding power, and the power between 1490 and 1800 shifted to countries or governments with great clout.

But when we started to discover machines, and when technology became an important aspect of the changing world, companies began to hold the power. During this period, if you wanted to be global, you really needed to be part of those big companies.

Modern power shifts: The era of communication

Using myself as an example, I started to become global when I joined Arthur Andersen because Arthur Andersen was a global company that existed all around the world. And then I moved to

Abbott. Being part of Abbott was very important to me because it provided access to the world and technology. Through the company, I was able to travel the world to get exposure to technology, information, training, and power.

But what happened next after 2000 was the optimisation of communication through the ability to browse and search for information. The era of communication became, I believe, the most important element in technology. In terms of internet browsing, the access to unlimited amounts of information at one's fingertips has provided a huge power to individuals, including me.

Since 2000, globalisation has taken on a different shape, the shape of the individual. The world is getting smaller and smaller, and has reached the individual. The power that used to be in the form of a global empire moved to the governments, then to the company, and now the power is with me. So, there is a big power shift. And every time the power shifts to another entity, the world takes a different shape.

In globalisation, when we say the world is getting smaller and smaller, it is because the power is taking on a different shape. And in today's world, the power is in the hands of individuals. Globalisation, in the eyes of the new generation, is about people, and nothing but people. When you say, I'm a global citizen, it refers to you really being a part of globalisation.

Let's illustrate this differently. To see how the world is getting smaller and smaller, it was flat before. In 1490, it became round. In 1800, it got smaller because it was in the hands of the company. Now, it's in the hands of the individuals, and it's extending to reach you.

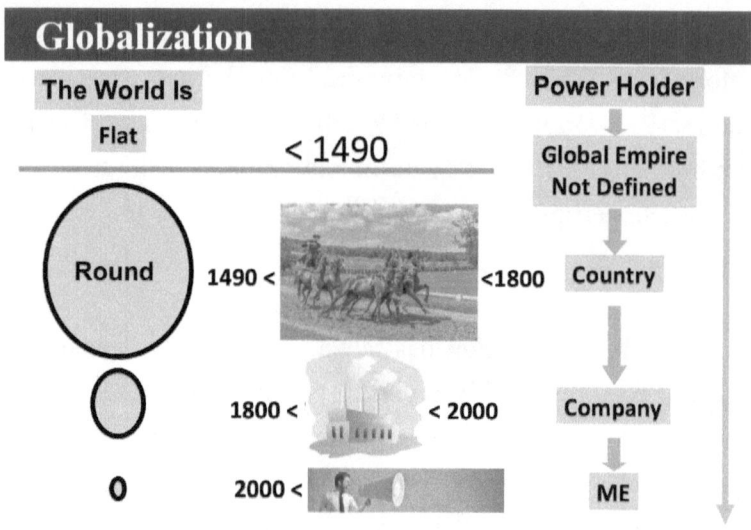

When I was researching on the internet for globalisation in images, I got different kinds of pictures that define globalisation in different ways. Some referred to communication, people talking with each other, people having the world in their minds, the world in your hand, holding the globe, but the globe is made of square, small squares, and in every square, there is a picture of a person. So, globalisation seemed more about communicating with people *(refer to below picture). If you think about it from the big picture, at the end of the day, it is about you, and it is about me.

Here, I want to use sports game as an analogy. We often see individuals shine within the team? And then, the individual becomes a symbol of the team. For example, when you think of Messi, you think of Barcelona; you don't think of Barcelona to think of Messi. That's how individuals are making a difference, not the group. So, if you think of sports, yes, sports is teamwork, provided every individual on the team is a star. Through globalisation, we have new forms of power. This is the power shift over eras.

I would love for you to think of the power and who holds the power, and be proud to hold it in your hand. If you imagine that you are able to look at the globalisation power in your hands, there is nothing stopping you from reaching out to people in any or even every part of the world.

But globalisation has some conditions that we need to meet, including loyalty shifts and expertise shifts.

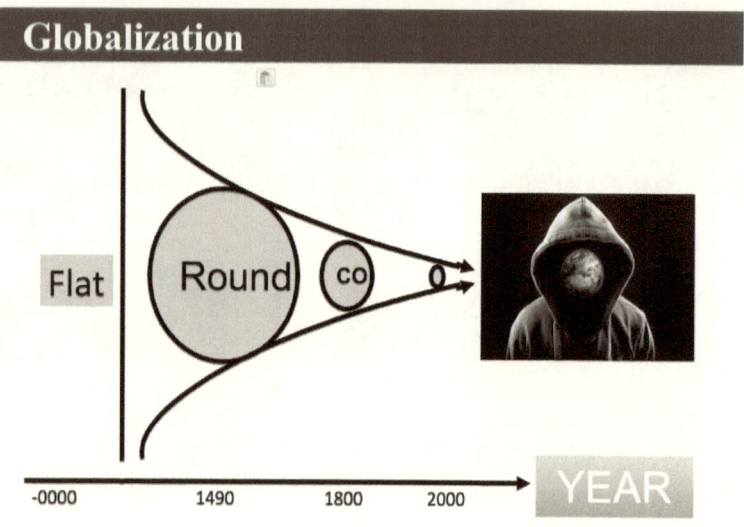

Loyalty shifts

You have a government, the enterprise, and you have the individuals. In globalisation, and through globalisation, we have a new form of loyalty.

There has been a shift, in particular, a loyalty shift. We spoke about who holds the power and now loyalty. During the government or the empire stage, people used to say, 'I belong to the Empire, I belong to the Roman Empire.' And then after that, when you meet people, and they want to introduce themselves, they will tell you, 'I work for XYZ.' For example, in the 1990s, when people asked me what I did, I would tell them, *I work for Abbott* or *I work for Arthur Andersen.*

And today, in the era of the individuals, when you ask people: What do you do? They will tell you *'At the moment I'm working "with"…'*

And here you have the equation, the equation of time, because when they say 'at the moment' it means it's very short in time, because they may change. And then they say: I'm working 'with,' not 'for.' It's a partnership, and there is an equal position. Looking at the angle of partnership, the angle of 'at the moment,' it means global people are free, free to work with whomever they want, free to operate with any entity, and free to change. They're not bound forever to anyone anymore.

So, to be free, you need to be qualified. There is another equation of qualification and freedom. People today need to look at the qualifications if they want to be global. And they need to have superior skills, either education or vocational education, which means technical skills. Irrespective of your profession, whether you are working in a corporation, for yourself, for a small entity or with the government, you need to be highly qualified to be able to be free and be global, move around different entities, take different initiatives, and be successful in the world.

Expertise shift

Being global means you need to be an expert. Having expertise in a specific field or niche field has become very important in today's world. To be considered global, you have to be qualified. And if you are qualified, you are free. This has created a big concern for corporations, as big companies today have a major concern with respect to retaining and attracting global individuals.

Global talent retention and attraction are indeed key issues for many corporations today. Here are a few examples that illustrate this concern.

Tech companies and AI specialists: The technology industry, particularly companies in AI, data science, and machine learning, compete fiercely for top talent. These individuals often have a global perspective, having been trained in top universities worldwide. Google, Facebook, Amazon, and other tech giants offer high salaries, great benefits, and interesting projects to retain and attract these talents. However, startups and other tech companies are also trying to lure these talents with the promise of equity, flexible work arrangements, and the chance to make a bigger impact.

Financial services and Blockchain experts: Blockchain technology has grown rapidly and has been integrated into various industries, especially the financial sector. Banks, hedge funds, and fintech firms are battling to attract and retain individuals who understand this technology. These professionals often have a global perspective, having witnessed the worldwide impact and applications of blockchain. Their ability to navigate the global landscape of blockchain regulations and innovations is highly prized.

Multinational corporations and global operations experts: Companies like Procter & Gamble, Coca-Cola, or Unilever, which operate in numerous markets worldwide, are constantly seeking individuals who understand global supply chains, market dynamics, and cultural nuances. These professionals need to be adept at managing and coordinating between different regions, and their skills are essential for these companies to operate smoothly on a global scale.

Pharmaceutical companies and global health experts: With global health issues like the COVID-19 pandemic, there is an increasing demand for professionals who understand global health challenges and can work on solutions that have a worldwide impact. Pharmaceutical companies like Pfizer, Moderna, and Johnson & Johnson are in dire need of these talents.

Consulting firms and global strategy experts: Consulting firms like McKinsey, BCG, and Deloitte, require employees who can provide advice to clients operating in multiple markets. These individuals need to understand global trends, diverse business environments, and how to strategise for international growth.

Companies are offering competitive compensation packages, career development opportunities, flexible work arrangements, diverse and inclusive work environments, and opportunities to work on challenging and impactful projects in order to retain and attract such global individuals. However, these professionals often have many opportunities available to them, and retaining them can be a significant challenge.

The whole world is changing today. Companies are revisiting their HR policies and incentives, and the big concern they have is how to retain staff and attract global individuals. And as such, retention is becoming a big challenge. We have noticed that the message of many entities or companies that have understood this shift of power change.

How has it changed?

When evaluating a company, one must ask: does its culture reflect the progressive realities of 2023? Or is it entrenched in archaic mindsets reminiscent of the 1700s? Just as companies need to modernise their operational ideologies, they must also ensure that their employees align with this forward-thinking mindset.

Today, it's imperative to discern the era to which a person's perspective belongs. Are they grounded in traditional values reminiscent of the 15th-century dictatorial culture, or are they more aligned with the industrial revolution, where power dynamics were skewed heavily towards companies? Most importantly, do they resonate with today's ethos that emphasises mutual respect, collaboration, and viewing employees as partners?

The current era demands mutual benefit. Gone are the days when companies could only flaunt their greatness. Now, to attract the finest talent, especially from younger generations, organisations need to highlight the symbiotic relationship: what's in it for both parties? This win-win narrative is paramount.

Consider modern sports teams as an analogy. Today's top athletes prioritise their skills and what they bring to the table. Their loyalty is driven by a balance of personal advancement and team success. Similarly, when hiring, companies must identify candidates with a progressive and global outlook. Such candidates not only bring qualifications to the table but also ensure they align with the company's evolving ethos.

As an exercise to better grasp this concept, make a list of individuals you know. Next to each name, try to gauge the era their mindset might belong to. This simple activity can provide profound insights into understanding and navigating the complex dynamics of today's professional world.

This version offers a more concise and structured take on the original paragraph, making the message clearer and more direct.

Level playing field

Globalisation today can be best described as the embodiment of freedom. The physical barriers once impeding movement are no longer relevant, with individuals freely transitioning between companies and countries. The digitisation of information has brought the world to our fingertips, allowing seamless access to vast resources from desktops, laptops, or handheld devices. Embracing globalisation benefits both individuals and humanity at large.

In today's interconnected world, anyone, even those in rural areas, can make substantial contributions to the global economy if equipped with the right qualifications and communication tools. India stands as a testament to this, with many of its towns serving as hubs for call centres and outsourced work due to a strong emphasis on education and cost-effectiveness.

Interestingly, someone from a small town in India with specialised skills might be more attuned to the global market than an individual in a metropolitan area who lacks the same expertise. This shift epitomises the idea that globalisation equates to freedom.

Modern behaviours, especially those observed among Millennials, accentuate the importance of freedom. For many, ownership has taken a backseat to experiences. They prioritise flexibility over permanence, renting over owning, exemplifying a global mindset where they feel they belong to the world, armed with the knowledge they possess.

Historically, entities like the Soviet Union resisted the tides of change, holding power close and centralising authority, eventually leading to their downfall. Similarly, companies that failed to decentralise power, adapt, and innovate have faded. Today's successful corporations champion individuality, nurture creativity, and foster an environment that welcomes innovation.

Globalisation is now intertwined with qualification. The world today demands individuals who cherish their freedom, are highly skilled, and recognise their influential role in this global era. The trajectory of power evolved from empires and kingdoms to companies, and now rests with empowered individuals, driven by technology and globalisation. As we navigate this era, it's imperative that organisations understand and embrace these power dynamics, valuing individual contributors who are shaping the future.

Conclusion

Globalisation, as illuminated through various historical shifts, represents a series of power transitions that have shaped our world. Historically, power migrated from empires to kingdoms, then from these kingdoms to influential companies during the industrial and technological revolutions. Presently, power resides with individuals, a testament to our increasingly connected, technology-driven world.

Assess yourself candidly in relation to your career, relationships, and personal aspirations. Ensure that your qualifications align with your ambition to be a truly global individual.

Building on the idea of self-assessment in the context of globalisation, the subsequent chapter emphasises the significance of knowledge sharing and fostering tolerance in professional settings. This approach will help to enhance the soft skills of team members.

7

LOVE & WORK

Creating a sharing environment while taking the first step

As we continue to navigate through the ever-changing landscapes of our interconnected world, one principle becomes increasingly significant: the power of sharing information. But sharing, much like a journey, begins with a single step. So, let's delve into the crucial role that taking that initial leap plays in shaping our global society. Let's explore why, now more than ever, stepping forward and sharing our knowledge is the cornerstone of progress in this era of rapid globalisation.

Let us explore the intricate connexion between fostering a nurturing environment conducive to sharing and taking the first step to initiate this process.

When we encounter the term 'sharing,' a host of interpretations spring to mind. Sharing could mean:

- Disseminating information among people
- Imparting knowledge or teaching
- Exchanging experiences for mutual benefits
- Creating shared moments
- Allocating resources or tools
- Dividing food
- Occupying shared spaces
- And many more possibilities

These varied interpretations can be broadly grouped under three categories:

1. Sharing moments (emotional): This involves sharing experiences, creating shared memories, or empathising with each other's feelings.
2. Sharing material (tangible): This refers to the sharing of physical objects, resources, or spaces.
3. Sharing information (educational): This encapsulates the exchange of knowledge, ideas, or information.

Given our focus on the professional sphere, the term 'sharing' often primarily evokes the third category: 'Sharing Information.'

We will concentrate on this particular category, tapping into the importance of fostering an ideal environment that encourages and facilitates the sharing of information in a healthy and motivational manner. We will explore strategies to stimulate intellectual exchange, inspire innovation, and create a collaborative learning culture within the professional space.

I-Sharing

Typically, the act of sharing information brings a sense of gratification. For instance, the experience of watching a movie in a cinema is often enhanced by the communal joy of sharing it with a larger audience.

The emotional outcome of sharing is fundamentally influenced by the intent behind such action. Generally, there are two primary motivations for sharing information:

A. Sharing out of obligation
B. Sharing driven by love and care

Sharing out of obligation can sometimes lead to discomfort and negative emotions. For instance, being compelled to share information during an investigation or under duress can be a stressful and demoralising experience. Conversely, when sharing is motivated by genuine care or love, it engenders a sense of happiness and motivation. Thus, we can represent these relationships as follows:

A. Sharing + Obligation = Discomfort
B. Sharing + Love & Care = Happiness

Therefore, the context and intent of sharing significantly impact the emotional response and overall experience of the sharing process.

A. Sharing by Obligation

Contrary to popular belief, sharing isn't always a voluntary act, particularly in a professional setting, where sharing is often a necessary part of our roles. Our contractual obligations compel us to share information, experience, and knowledge. Moreover, we are frequently required to demonstrate leadership behaviours to our colleagues.

As previously noted, voluntary sharing can bring joy, while obligatory sharing might not evoke the same response. However, that isn't always the case.

Take parenting, for example. Parents have a duty to share knowledge, guidance, and resources with their children. Though this act of sharing springs from obligation, it is often intertwined with deep love and care. This combination transforms an otherwise duty-bound task into a rewarding, joyful experience. Here, even though sharing is borne out of obligation, the blend of love and care imbues it with a sense of fulfilment and happiness. It can be regarded as the ultimate level of sharing, one that transcends mere duty and becomes a profound expression of care and affection. (Refer to graphic 1).

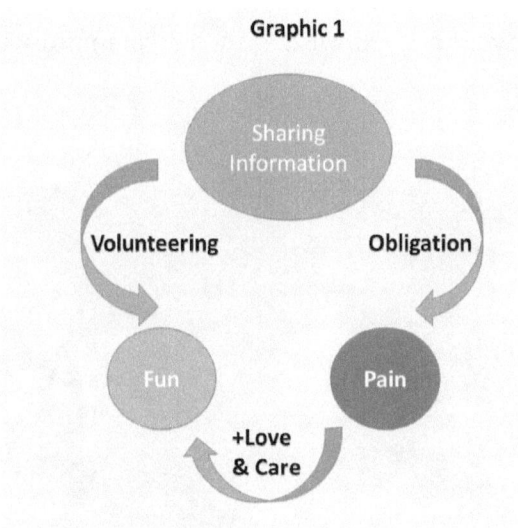

Graphic 1

B. Sharing By Love & Care

While sharing driven by love is certainly valuable and essential, it might not always be consistent, as it hinges on personal feelings. When sharing is coupled with a sense of obligation, it not only becomes more credible and consistent but also improves the quality of the shared content.

People often feel more at ease receiving information when it's disseminated through a sharing process fuelled by both obligation and love. This blend of duty and affection creates a trust-rich environment where shared knowledge is perceived as reliable and meaningful, enhancing the overall communication dynamics within a team or community. (Refer to graphic 2).

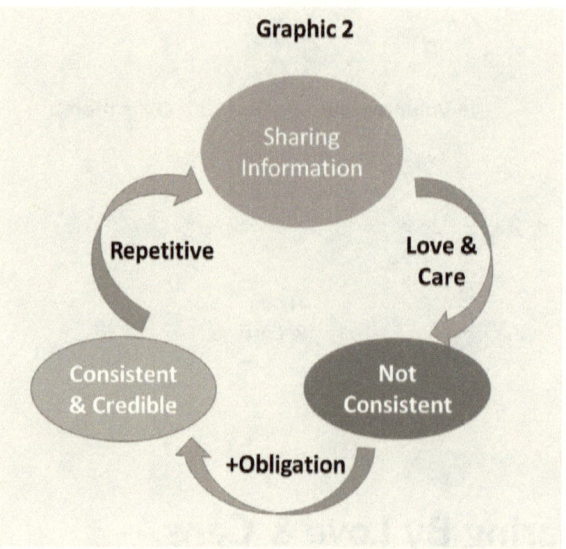

To construct a comprehensive understanding, there's one more element to add to the mix of love and obligation: that is a positive work environment. The amalgamation of these three elements: love, obligation, and a positive work environment, breeds an 'ideal' setting for sharing. This harmonious trinity facilitates open communication, promotes collaboration, and enhances overall productivity, thus establishing an exemplary platform for information sharing and collective growth. (Refer to graphic 3).

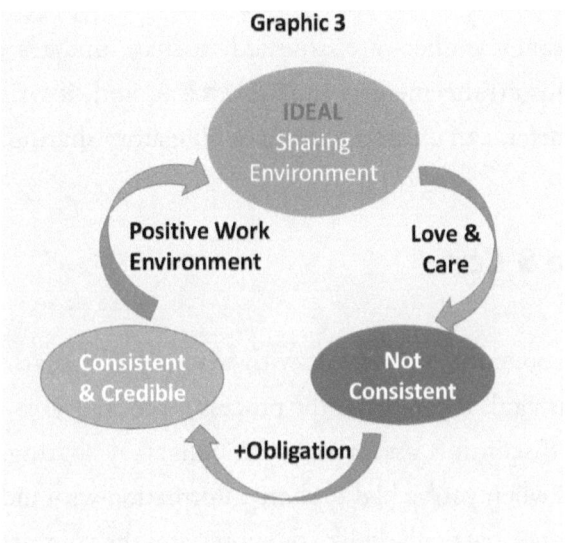

Pillars of an ideal sharing environment

A. Obligation:

This commitment must embody the following characteristics:

A. Equitable, fostering a win-win situation for all parties involved.
B. Preferably articulated in writing for clarity and accountability.
C. Clear, bidirectional expectations, elucidating what is anticipated from you as a giver and from the contract-bound party as a receiver.

D. Widely accepted and adopted by all participants involved.

For instance, a team leader could establish regular meetings where team members are expected to share updates on their tasks. This arrangement is equitable, clear, and, if written in a team charter, can create a culture of obligatory sharing.

B. Love & Care:

Caring about the individuals with whom you're sharing information is vital. It can make the process more enjoyable, alleviating any discomfort associated with obligatory sharing. Reflect on times when you've had to share information with individuals you may not particularly like or appreciate, the contrast is quite stark.

For example, a mentor genuinely caring for their mentee's growth will find joy in sharing their knowledge and experience, enhancing the overall mentoring relationship.

C. Positive Work Environment:

Passion for your work plays a crucial role in cultivating a positive work environment. As a leader, your contribution to this positive atmosphere is significant. This will be further explored later in the chapter when we dig into the importance of taking the first step.

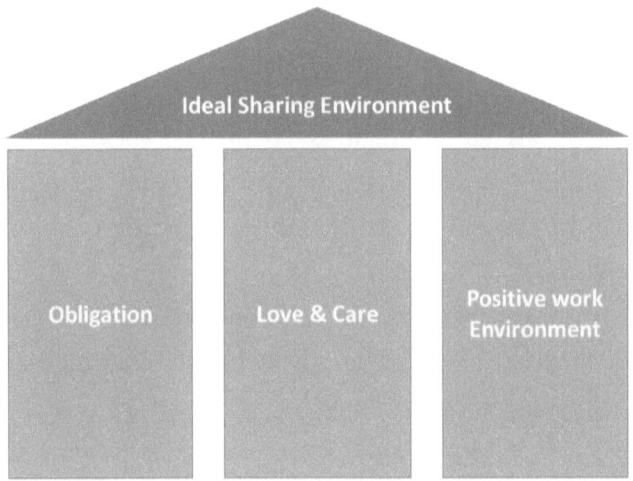

Consider a scenario where a manager encourages open dialogue, celebrates successes, and promotes a collaborative culture. Such an environment would foster a positive work atmosphere conducive to effective and joyful information sharing.

The energising power of sharing in professional environments

Let's take a look again at Graph-1, which illustrates the correlation between Obligation, Love, Energy, and Productivity.

In a professional context, sharing is often a mandate rather than a choice. However, even if you harbour love and care as intrinsic aspects of your personality and work ethic, you still need an optimal environment to leverage your sharing potential to the fullest. This conducive setting is your workplace environment.

- In such an environment, sharing becomes more fluid. The more you share, the happier you feel. It initiates a cycle where you need the energy to boost your sharing productivity.
- A significant factor in any environment is the infusion of love and care. It is a catalyst for healthy and high-quality sharing outcomes.
- Keep in mind that we all have an obligation to share in various facets of our professional lives, so we may as well strive to make it more enjoyable and less burdensome.

In Graph-4, you'll see that the energy required for sharing drops significantly as the factor of love and care increases. When sharing is driven purely by obligation, the energy expenditure is much higher. However, as the energy requirement lessens, your ability to produce more volume increases, thereby enhancing your overall productivity.

As you can see, the energy factor plays a pivotal role since it directly impacts productivity. For example, a teacher who loves and cares for their students will expend less energy while teaching (sharing knowledge) than one who views teaching purely as an obligation. Consequently, the former's productivity, in terms of the quality and quantity of teaching, is likely to be higher.

While creating a perfect sharing environment is the responsibility of all employees, this primarily falls to the organisation's leaders. It is important to develop diagnostic tools that enable management to measure the level of the sharing environment.

A key question that should always be considered is, 'As a leader, what should I do to create and maintain such a desired environment?' In the subsequent sections, I will discuss some crucial factors to focus on and introduce some measurement tools in this regard.

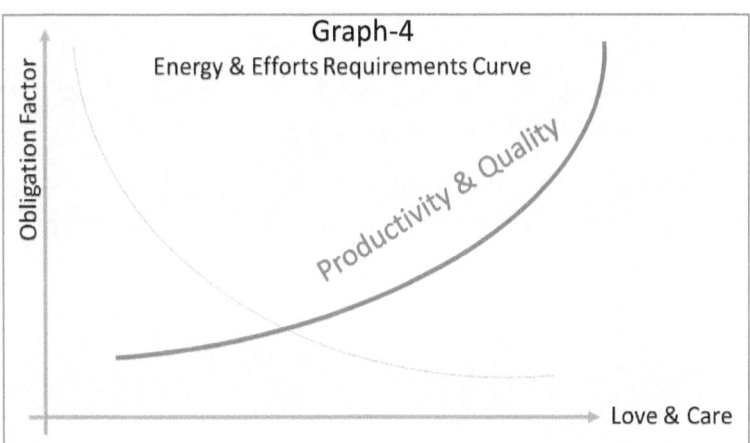

Measurement tools: Velocity

In this segment, we introduce an innovative concept that borrows from the realm of physics: 'velocity,' with the aim of leveraging it as a metric in evaluating a sharing environment.

In physics, velocity is a primary determinant of an object's speed and position. It's essentially defined as the distance travelled by an object per unit of time or, alternatively, the displacement of an object over a given period.

In our context, we redefine velocity as the ratio of the amount of information shared to the energy expended in disseminating that information.

Sharing Velocity = Productivity / Energy

In this equation, 'productivity' serves as a measure of the volume of knowledge being shared, while 'energy' represents the quality of the environment conducive to sharing. If more energy is required to share information, it signifies an unfavourable environment, consequently leading to a decline in the sharing velocity.

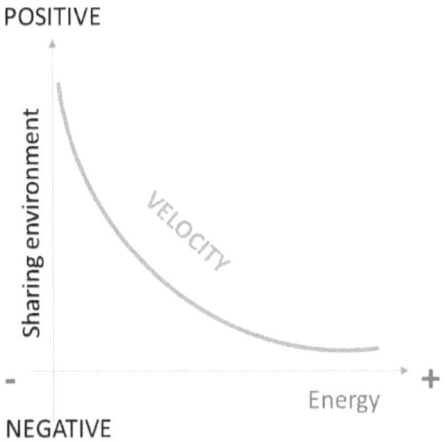

Measuring productivity and energy

Productivity

Productivity can vary from one company to another. It can be measured by calculating a weighted average score resulting from the responses to various questions, such as

- How many projects are you working on as a team member?
- How many unfinished projects are you currently involved in?
- How many projects have been completed but delivered late?
- How many projects were finished on time?
- Are you receiving adequate training?
- Does your leader provide you with the necessary tools to complete your projects?

- Is your team properly equipped to support you with your projects?

In terms of productivity, the higher your score, the better your performance.

Energy

Like productivity, the level of energy can vary from company to company. It can be measured by calculating a weighted average score from the responses to different questions, such as:

A. Does your supervisor provide the encouragement needed to complete your tasks?
B. Does your team offer support when you're working on a project?
C. Is there a level of dissatisfaction or complaint within the team regarding the work?
D. Do team members often work extra hours?
E. Do you sense passion in your team members when working with them?
F. Do you conduct periodic feedback programmes or surveys to receive anonymous feedback?
G. Is your employee turnover rate higher than average?
H. Are your team members appropriately rewarded?

I. Are there programmes in place that recognise team members who take incremental steps in sharing knowledge and information?

In terms of energy, the lower your score, the better your environment.

Note: It's important to balance the total scores to ensure accurate scoring for velocity. This provides a more interpretive measurement.

Velocity calculation example: Company A

- Sharing Velocity = $\dfrac{\text{Productivity}}{\text{Energy}}$

Company A	Score	Weight	Theoretical top score	Score	%
In productivity the higher you score the better you are 1 bad 10 excellent					
1. Evaluate the number of projects you work on as a team member	8	1	10	8	80%
2. Evaluate the non-achieved projects you are working on	6	2	20	12	60%
3. evaluate Amount of projects achieved but late	3	1	10	3	30%
4. Number of projects you finish on time	5	2	20	10	50%
5. Are you receiving enough training	4	1	10	4	40%
6. Does your leader provides you with enough tools to achieve your projects	4	1	10	4	40%
7. Is your team properly equipped to support you on your projects	5	1	10	5	50%
8. Are you exceeding your plan targets	5	2	20	10	50%
9. Is your company gaining market share	3	1	10	3	30%
Total Productivity			120	59	49%
In energy the lowest you score the better you are 10 bad 11 excellent					
1. Does your supervisor provides encouragement to achieve your task	9	2	20	18	90%
2. Does your team supports you while working on a project	7	2	20	14	70%
3. Are the team complaining about the work	6	2	20	12	60%
4. Do they put in extra hours while working	3	1	10	5	50%
5. Do you feel and sense the passion in the team members while working with you	8	1	10	8	80%
6. Do you run a periodic feedback program or surveys to receive anonymous feedback	10	1	10	10	100%
7. Is your employee turnover above normal	8	1	10	8	80%
8. Is your team properly rewarded	9	1	10	9	90%
9. Do you have programs that remunerate team members who exercise incremental steps	9	1	10	9	90%
Total Energy		12	120	93	78%

Velocity = 59/93=0.63

Interpretation: The sharing velocity in this company is low below 1. We are spending too much energy to generate a 49 per cent outcome as shown in total productivity.

When velocity is below 1, it means we need to take action.

Let us remember that velocity is a measure taken at a certain period. It is crucial we periodically measure velocity through official surveys and watch the trend.

Velocity calculation example: Company B

- Sharing Velocity = $\dfrac{\text{Productivity}}{\text{Energy}}$

124 PIQUE YOUR PATH TO ACHIEVEMENTS

Company B	Score	Weight	Theoretical top score	Weighted Score	%
In productivity the higher you score the better you are 1 bad 10 excellent					
1. Evaluate the number of projects you work on as a team member	8	1	10	8	80%
2. Evaluate the non-achieved projects you are working on	9	2	20	18	90%
3. evaluate Amount of projects achieved but late	9	1	10	9	90%
4. Number of projects you finish on time	8	2	20	16	80%
5. Are you receiving enough training	7	1	10	7	70%
6. Does your leader provides you with enough tools to achieve your projects	8	1	10	8	80%
7. Is your team properly equipped to support you on your projects	9	1	10	9	90%
8. Are you exceeding your plan targets	8	2	20	16	80%
9. Is your company gaining market share	8	1	10	8	80%
Total Productivity			120	99	83%
In energy the lowest you score the better you are 10 bad 11 excellent					
1. Does your supervisor provides encouragement to achieve your task	2	2	20	4	20%
2. Does your team supports you while working on a project	3	2	20	6	30%
3. Are the team complaining about the work	1	2	20	2	10%
4. Do they put in extra hours while working	1	1	10	5	50%
5. Do you feel and sense the passion in the team members while working with you	2	1	10	2	20%
6. Do you run a periodic feedback program or surveys to receive anonymous feedback	1	1	10	1	10%
7. Is your employee turnover above normal	3	1	10	3	30%
8. Is your team properly rewarded	5	1	10	5	50%
9. Do you have programs that remunerate team members who exercise incremental steps	4	1	10	4	40%
Total Energy		12	120	32	27%

Velocity = 99/32=3.1

Interpretation: The sharing velocity in this company is high, over 1. We are spending lower energy to generate 83 per cent outcome as shown in the total productivity table.

When velocity is above 1, it means we need to continue building on the momentum.

Let us remember that velocity is a measure taken at a certain period. It is crucial that we periodically measure velocity through official surveys and watch the trend.

Velocity trend

In this section, I wish to underscore the value of evaluating trends in velocity measurements, rather than focusing on isolated readings.

As illustrated in the figure titled Sharing Velocity, serves as our baseline for velocity measurements. From this, it's evident that company A shows a trend of improvement, while company B displays a downward trajectory, even though company A initially held a much superior position.

While individual numbers are not to be overlooked, the main emphasis when comparing the velocity of two teams, or companies, should be placed on recognising and interpreting the overall trend.

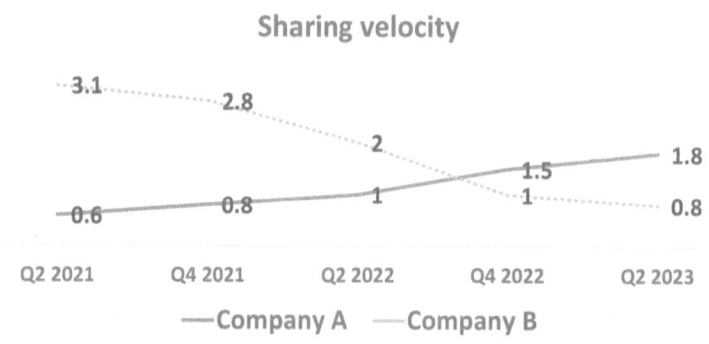

The roles of giver and receiver

Building on the prior paragraph's discussion of feedback, this one too, highlights the importance of dual participation. In any sharing activity, two primary roles emerge: the giver and the receiver. Together, they bear the responsibility of nurturing an environment that facilitates the effortless exchange of information and knowledge.

As illustrated in the graph below, each party has a pivotal role to play. The giver needs to share information effectively, while the receiver needs to offer valuable feedback. If either party ceases to fulfil their role, the sharing cycle is interrupted, and the sharing activity is negatively impacted.

For a successful sharing activity, both the giver and receiver should experience an equal level of satisfaction. This equilibrium will result in high productivity and velocity, thereby maximising the outcome of their joint efforts.

Consider a training scenario. If the trainer isn't conveying the information adequately, the attendees' level of engagement will inevitably decrease, thereby impacting overall productivity. In this instance, while the satisfaction of the giver (trainer) might be high, it likely won't align with the lower satisfaction of the receivers (trainees). This mismatch can result in a significant loss in the overall outcome.

In such a situation, it falls on the giver to analyse what might have gone wrong. Concurrently, it is the receivers' responsibility to provide honest and objective feedback. A significant question that arises here is: Who should take the initiative toward accurate diagnosis?

In the following sections, we will discuss the crucial importance of taking the first step and the potential outcomes that it may yield.

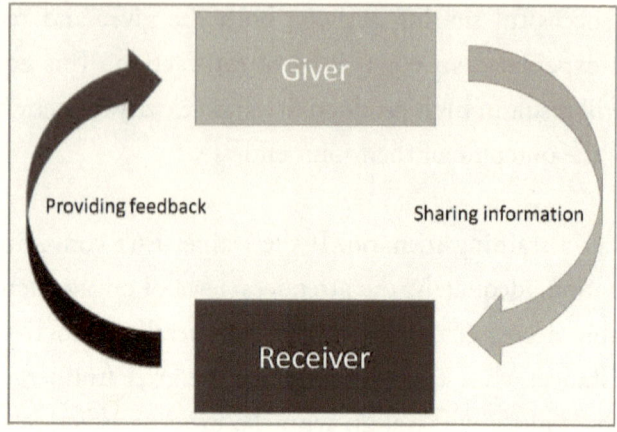

The first step

When you sense that the sharing environment is accompanied by complaints and information flow is hindered, it's a sign that your company or department may be experiencing the formation of silos. To address this, it is essential to take the initiative and start investigating the reasons behind this issue. Begin by asking yourself some critical questions:

What is my role in this department?

A. Am I primarily a receiver, a giver, or both?
B. Am I receiving regular feedback, and have I taken the time to analyse it?

After evaluating your role and responsibilities, don't hesitate to take the first step and approach your counterparts, whether individuals or groups. Request their feedback and concerns about the situation. Avoid waiting for others to act, as taking the first step is vital in creating a healthy environment for sharing. Shifting the blame onto others is not a solution and will only drain your company, department, and yourself, of energy and time, thereby reducing velocity. Remember, in such a situation, you share part of the responsibility for the created issues, just like in a shared car accident. When the sharing environment falters, someone needs to take the first step, and you can be that person. Don't miss the opportunity.

Barriers to taking the first step

There are several reasons why people might be reluctant to take the first step:

a) Ego
b) Fear
c) Concern about the counterpart's reaction
d) Fear of being seen as guilty
e) Resistance to taking responsibility
f) Lack of interest or apathy
g) Feeling that it's not their business or role

h) Blaming others
i) Belief that they will leave the situation soon
j) Apathy or indifference

Despite these barriers, it's crucial to remember the importance of the first step in fostering a healthy environment for sharing.

The power of the first step

In the professional realm, those who occupy positions of greater authority or responsibility are typically expected to make the initial move. Doing so allows them to attain two significant assets:

Respect: When leaders take the initiative, they portray themselves as caring and proactive individuals. They demonstrate their commitment to their team, showing that they are prepared to take the first step not just out of obligation, but out of a genuine desire to address and resolve issues.

Increased tolerance: Taking the initial step generally leads to more cooperation, flexibility, and appreciation from others. In managing conflicts, those who initiate the first step tend to gain more respect and recognition, even if they don't completely accomplish their objective. The secret to success hinges on good manners and proactivity.

Promoting an 'Initiative-Driven Environment'

As a team leader, your duty involves cultivating an environment where taking the initiative is both promoted and appreciated. Each time someone makes an effort to reach out to you, don't wait, seize the opportunity and react accordingly. Remember, the key to earning respect and love from others is in taking the first step earnestly and considerately.

This process isn't merely about problem-solving; it's about fostering a culture of proactive engagement, demonstrating the values of respect, tolerance, and open communication. Such an environment enables everyone to feel comfortable stepping forward, which contributes to creating a healthier, more cooperative, and effective workplace.

Consider the example of a sports team. The coach, holding the highest authority, often takes the first step by setting clear expectations, providing feedback, and maintaining open communication lines. This action invites team members to feel comfortable voicing their thoughts, asking questions, and offering suggestions. They understand that their contribution is valued, and this fosters a culture of initiative and cooperation.

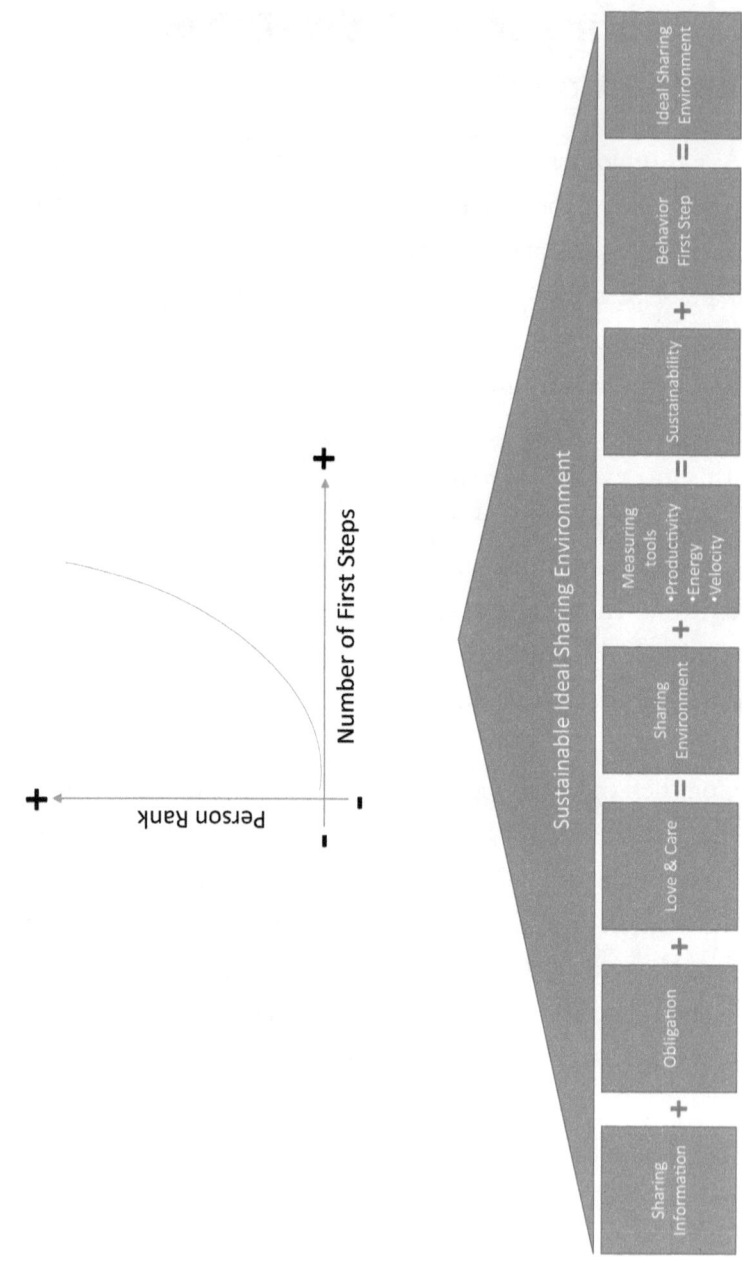

Summary

In navigating our interconnected world, information sharing stands as a crucial principle, beginning with a single step. This chapter explores the concept of sharing in its myriad forms, from exchanging experiences and knowledge to allocating resources, with a particular focus on the exchange of information in the professional sphere.

The pivotal question I urge you to ponder upon as we conclude this chapter is: where do you see yourself in this discourse? Are you a spectator or an active participant? Are you sharing knowledge and taking initiative? Are you fostering an environment that encourages sharing and taking the first step in your organisation?

I implore you not to remain a bystander. There's limited room for passengers in this dynamic world, what's truly sought after are genuine leaders. Leaders who disseminate information, who aren't afraid to take the first step, who actively work towards creating a thriving environment.

So, be among those who seize the initiative. Propel yourself to the forefront and you'll find yourself winning not just battles, but wars.

In the upcoming chapter, we'll delve into the concept of competition, exploring it from multiple angles. We will discuss how to compete effectively, establish a competitive advantage, and, importantly, how to respect the rules of competition.

8

COMPETITION

From the biblical conflict between Cain and Abel to the modern rivalry between Pepsi and Coca-Cola, competition has always been a staple in human history. Yet, it is much more than an innate instinct; it's a vital driver that pushes us toward betterment, innovation, and growth. But to harness the power of competition, one must first understand its intricacies. Let us venture into the labyrinth of competition, illuminating its aspects, influences, and the necessary tools for successful navigation. Through the lens of personal growth, corporate battles, and the legendary piano duel from 'The Legend of 1900,' we explore the compelling dance of competition and its indispensable role in our journey toward success.

Competition has existed since the dawn of humankind, dating back to the biblical tale of Cain and Abel. Stemming from jealousy and the desire to win God's favour, Cain's act against his brother symbolises the potential destructive power of unchecked competition. Since then, competition, driven by human ambition for greater benefits and power, has evolved and manifested in countless forms.

What are the key ingredients for competition?

For competition to exist, we need at least three elements:

a) A minimum of two parties
b) A common target, customer, or audience that both parties are competing for
c) Operating within the same field or in complementary areas

Defining competitors

Competitors can be defined as a group of individuals or companies striving to reach the same target within the same sphere. They can be broadly classified into three categories:

a) Direct competition
b) Indirect competition
c) Potential or future competition

We will be looking at the impact of competition on individuals rather than companies, although corporate examples will be used as analogies for clearer understanding.

Why we need to compete

Competition is an inherent aspect of life that touches every sphere, personal or professional. From birth, we're brought up in a world where competition is ingrained: in sports, academics, professional endeavours, and in the constant comparisons we draw with others. Embracing competition is vital, as it's a fundamental part of our journey toward success. Competition pushes us to improve, stretch our limits, and achieve more.

For instance, the ongoing rivalry between Apple and Samsung has spurred innovative and advanced products, increasing customer satisfaction. Similarly, competition between artists leads to exceptional music, and among athletes, it elevates the sports we enjoy.

However, it's essential to understand that the purpose of competition should not be to obliterate your competition. There's a danger that in doing so, you may inadvertently harm yourself.

Recognising the competition: An unveiling exercise in self-improvement

Identifying your competition, whether in business or personal endeavours, is an essential first step in the pursuit of success. Just as a ship's captain navigates the vast ocean by understanding the currents and weather patterns, you must chart your course by identifying and understanding your competitors.

Competitors are not solely limited to those within your immediate sphere; they may emerge from peripheral areas, often undetected, until they pose a significant challenge. This subtle shift in the competitive landscape, like an undercurrent, can steer you off your intended path if not identified early on.

For instance, consider the iconic rivalry between Pepsi and Coca-Cola. These beverage titans, so focused on outperforming one another, overlooked a more subtle competitor emerging - the shift towards healthier choices, epitomised by water. Caught in the throes of their direct competition, these giants were blindsided by this broader market shift.

Thus, recognising your competition is not just about identifying direct rivals. It is an exercise in broadening your perspective, capturing the entire landscape in which you operate. This requires an understanding of direct, indirect, and potential competition, each contributing to the overall competitive environment.

This principle is equally applicable in the realm of personal development. Your competitors may not always be your peers in the professional field. They could be individuals embodying qualities, skills, or achievements that you aspire to. In this context, identifying your competition is not about kindling envy or malice; rather, it is a tool for self-assessment and motivation.

Viewing competition healthily can make it a catalyst for personal growth. Instead of a threatening rival, your competitor could be a benchmark for your own progress, a source of inspiration, or a learning opportunity.

Being aware of your competition keeps you proactive, ready to adapt, and continually striving for self-improvement. This awareness fuels your drive to be the best version of yourself, enabling you to maintain your competitive edge in every aspect of life. In the unfolding narrative of your journey to success, recognising and understanding your competition is an essential chapter.

Negative competition

In this context, let's consider a compelling example from the film, 'The Legend of 1900.' This film tells the story of an orphaned child who grows into a prodigious pianist aboard an ocean liner. A powerful scene from this movie, 'The Piano Duel,' exemplifies the destructive nature of competition when combined with arrogance and overconfidence.

The scene unfolds between the protagonist, 1900, and a well-known jazz pianist, Jelly Roll Morton. Overflowing with arrogance, Morton cannot stand the rising popularity of the young pianist and challenges him to a musical duel, aiming to assert his dominance.

The duel consists of three rounds, with Morton exuding overconfidence and belittling his opponent throughout. However, 1900 chooses to focus on the joy of competition and the audience's entertainment.

During the final round, Morton's arrogance reaches a climax, and he exhibits demeaning behaviour towards 1900, who, in turn, decides to showcase his true skills.

The result is Morton's utter defeat and 1900's triumphant victory. The audience, quickly shifting their loyalties, celebrates the new champion, leaving Morton to face his downfall alone. Reference:

Legend of the 1900s Piano Duel

https://youtu.be/5USKFpk2E3Y

This scene mirrors real-life scenarios where emerging technologies disrupt existing ones. Customer loyalty is, in reality, linked to the quality of a product or service. For example, the shift from Nokia to Apple, or from Kodak to digital cameras, illustrates that customers lean towards the best available option.

Therefore, the question arises, who is to blame: the audience for shifting their loyalty or Morton for his arrogant approach? The audience cannot be blamed, as their loyalty was never to Morton per se, but to his music. As soon as a better performer appeared, their loyalty naturally shifted. Thus, it's crucial to remember that, in any competitive environment, loyalty follows the best offering, whether that's a product, service, or individual.

How to compete

'Mastering the Art of Competition: A Guide to Effective Competitive Strategies'

In the vast landscape of competition, understanding the environment is only half the battle. To emerge triumphant, you must also be adept at managing your position within that landscape. This involves adopting and maintaining effective strategies that not only elevate your performance but also build resilience against potential threats. The following section outlines a five-step guide to compete effectively, underpinned by continuous self-assessment, understanding of competitors, optimal resource utilisation, integrity, and mutual respect. We will also tackle a practical example, illustrating these principles in the context of a software development company.

To compete effectively, you should:

1. Continually assess your offerings, comparing them against industry-leading standards to identify areas for improvement.
2. Understand who your actual and potential competitors are. Regularly analyse the market trends to keep track of current competitors and anticipate future ones.
3. Leverage all available resources and tools to gain a competitive edge. This can include anything from technology and human resources to networking opportunities and marketing strategies.
4. Maintain modesty and integrity in your dealings and promises. This not only fosters trust but also helps to exceed client expectations, thus enhancing your reputation.
5. Show respect towards your competitors. Healthy competition promotes innovation, improves products or services, and benefits the industry as a whole.

Let's take an example of a software development company. This company should keep an eye on the market trends, upcoming technologies, and what its competitors are working on (Point 2). It needs to continually update its software and skills to match the industry-leading standards (Point 1). It can use the latest software development tools, attend tech conferences, or organise internal training sessions to improve its offerings (Point 3). While selling its software, it should not over-promise the features. Instead, it should focus on delivering more than what it promised (Point 4). Finally, respecting its competitors, it could collaborate with them for larger projects or mutually beneficial initiatives (Point 5).

Conclusion

This chapter has looked into the multidimensional aspects of competition, dissecting its characteristics, necessity, and the art of harnessing it effectively. Tracing the origins of competition from biblical times to contemporary corporate battles, by unpacking competition's influence in our personal lives and professional fields, the chapter highlights the importance of correctly identifying our competitors.

Without competition, our existence may stagnate; we innovate and improve primarily spurred by the spirit of competition. It serves as the catalyst for enhancing our offerings and bolstering customer satisfaction. To master the art of competition, it's essential to adhere to its fundamental rules: be prepared, stay agile, and embrace the constant challenge.

Don't miss the enlightening case study in the next chapter featuring Boeing and Airbus. It's a fascinating example of two titans clashing in the aviation industry's competitive arena, providing valuable insights into the dynamics of competition at its fiercest.

9

PHILOSOPHY-DRIVEN STRATEGY

The word 'strategy' is a common part of our vocabulary, a topic often discussed and debated. Strategy has been integral to human existence and progress since time immemorial. It serves as our roadmap, guiding us toward our desired destination. We cannot live or operate without a strategy; even when one appears to be absent, the lack of strategy itself becomes the strategy.

Whether times of war or peace, prosperity or poverty, under ordinary or challenging circumstances, or at any stage of our lives or businesses, having a strategy is essential.

The objective of this chapter, however, is not to guide you on how to write a strategy, as that has been extensively discussed, explained, and analysed elsewhere. Instead, I aim to highlight the importance of letting philosophy drive strategy, not vice versa. I also want to underscore the necessity of adhering to specific steps when formulating your strategy. While I will be using business examples to illustrate these points, I encourage you to apply these concepts on a personal level, too. Lastly, I aim to provide a simple methodology that will enable you to craft your philosophy, leading to your strategy.

Philosophy

The Last Two Decades: Boeing vs Airbus

In aviation, there is no competition more fierce than that between Boeing and Airbus. Over the past two decades, these two industry giants have adopted starkly different strategies, each reflective of their underlying business philosophies.

Boeing, with the launch of the 787 Dreamliner, chose to focus on 'point to point' travel. Its goal was to provide carriers with a fuel-efficient aircraft capable of long-haul flights, thus enabling direct routes between cities and bypassing the need for stopovers. This strategy was informed by its belief that customers valued the ability to travel from one specific location to another without interruption.

On the other hand, Airbus, with its A380 double-deck aircraft, pursued a strategy centred around 'moving people.' Its massive airliner, the largest passenger aircraft in the world, was designed to transport a large number of passengers in one flight, thereby enhancing the economies of scale for airlines. Airbus's philosophy is rooted in its belief that it needed a solution to transport as many passengers as possible from one destination to another.

In essence, Boeing's philosophy behind its strategy was 'Point to Point,' while Airbus's philosophy was 'Moving People.' These contrasting philosophies led the two corporations to invest heavily in research, development, and manufacturing to produce innovative solutions tailored to their respective visions.

When one of the CEOs was asked which strategy would prove successful, his response was, 'Customers will decide.' This statement underscores the fact that a strategy is meaningless if it does not resonate with customers or create a competitive advantage. Ultimately, it's the customers' needs and preferences that determine the success or failure of a business strategy.

Below is an illustration of these two philosophies and their resulting outcomes.

Source:
Point-to-Point Distribution Model. How Does it Work?
by Murray Phillips, Dec 07 2022
An Analysis of the Competitive Actions of Boeing and Airbus in the Aerospace Industry Based on the Competitive Dynamics Model
J. Open Innov. Technol. Mark. Complex. 2021, 7(3), 192; https://doi.org/10.3390/joitmc7030192
Received: 19 July 2021 / Revised: 9 August 2021 / Accepted: 11 August 2021 / Published: 31 August 2021

BOEING

Point to Point
Efficient planes
Lower fuel consumption
Engines capable of extended operation
Reduced noise levels
Enhanced passenger comfort
Substituting aluminium with fibre materials

787 Dreamliner

AIRBUS

Moving People
Big planes
Bigger engines
Spacious first and business class

A380 Double-Deck

It's crucial to establish a guiding philosophy before crafting your strategy. This philosophy should be concise and easy to remember, encapsulating the core principles that drive your strategic decisions. Although this philosophy may be interpreted slightly differently across various departments or individuals, it should ultimately create a coherent, unified vision towards the desired strategic goal.

Boeing and Airbus, two industrial giants, were able to condense their respective strategic philosophies into two distinct phrases: 'Point to Point' for Boeing and 'Moving People' for Airbus. These simple, potent philosophies have guided significant decisions, investments, and innovations in their companies.

Likewise, regardless of the size or scope of your endeavour, you too can encapsulate your strategic vision in a few meaningful words. Having a clear, concise philosophy can be a powerful tool in guiding your strategy and ensuring everyone involved is aligned towards a common goal.

Strategy roadmap

When it comes to formulating a comprehensive strategy, you'll want to follow these steps:

1- Identifying your core philosophy: This involves determining the key principles and beliefs that will guide your actions and decisions. The philosophy is your anchor, the non-negotiable essence of who you are as an individual or organisation.

2- Establishing strategic directions: Based on your philosophy, chart out the path you want to take. What are the broad objectives or goals you want to achieve? These directions will give you a sense of direction and purpose.

3- Validating the strategy: After you have a preliminary strategy in place, it's important to validate it. This could involve soliciting feedback from various stakeholders, conducting market research or running small-scale pilot projects to test the feasibility of your strategic plans.

4- Aligning the strategy across departments: Once the strategy has been validated, ensure that it is clearly communicated and understood across all departments in your organisation. Everyone should be on the same page about what the strategy is and what their role in it is.

5- Commencing implementation: The final step is to put the strategy into action. This is where the real work begins. Remember, a strategy is not a static document, it's a living, breathing guide that should be continually revisited and revised as necessary.

Let's consider a hypothetical tech startup. They might identify their core philosophy as 'Innovate to Simplify.' Their strategic directions could be focused on developing user-friendly tech solutions. They might validate their strategy through customer surveys and focus groups. They would then ensure that all teams, from product development to marketing, understand this strategy and know their part in it. Finally, they would begin implementing their strategy, constantly reviewing and revising their approach based on market feedback and internal progress.

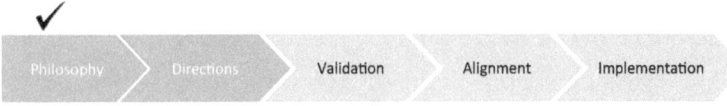

Ascertain your philosophy

To ascertain your philosophy, you need to undertake the task of identifying your options, understanding your unique value proposition, and determining your competitive edge. In other words, it necessitates introspection and exploration into who you are, what you intend to provide, and how your offerings differentiate you from others in the market.

Let's consider the example of an up-and-coming eco-friendly clothing brand.

To determine its philosophy, the brand must first identify its options: what kind of sustainable materials it can use, which demographic it will target, what kind of styles and designs it wants to specialise in.

Next, it needs to establish its unique value proposition. This could include offering clothing items made from 100 per cent sustainable materials, promoting ethical labour practices, or creating unique, high-quality designs that don't compromise on style for sustainability.

Finally, the brand has to pinpoint its competitive edge. Perhaps it has a unique supply chain that ensures the ethical sourcing and production of materials, or maybe it employs a talented in-house design team with an exceptional knack for predicting fashion trends.

Through this process of identifying options, articulating a value proposition, and recognising a competitive advantage, the clothing brand crafts a compelling philosophy that will guide its strategy moving forward. This philosophy might be something like 'Sustainable Style, Ethically Made', a succinct phrase that captures its essence, what it offers, and how it stands out.

SOURCE: OPEN SOURCE INSPIRED FROM VARIOUS BUSINESS INSTITUTION

Identifying your philosophy is just the beginning. Let's delve deeper into the subsequent steps to develop your comprehensive strategy.

1. Option - Who am I?
   This step focuses on understanding how you want to be perceived by others and what you stand for. It involves defining your core values, mission, and purpose. By clarifying your identity, you create a strong foundation for your strategy. For example, a tech company may identify itself as an innovative

and customer-centric organisation aiming to revolutionise the industry with cutting-edge solutions.

2. Value proposition
   Once you know who you are, the next step is to determine what you offer and why it matters. Your value proposition defines the unique benefits and solutions you provide to your customers. It's about understanding your target audience's needs and positioning your products or services to fulfil those needs better than anyone else. For instance, a fast-food restaurant might emphasise its quick service and affordable prices as its value proposition.

3. Competitive advantage
   With a clear value proposition, you can identify what sets you apart from your competitors. Your competitive advantage could be based on various factors, such as superior technology, lower costs, exceptional customer service, or exclusive partnerships. This advantage positions you as the preferred choice in the market. For example, an online retailer might boast a wide selection of products, fast shipping, and a user-friendly website as its competitive edge.

You lay the groundwork for your strategy by effectively addressing these three components. Your philosophy becomes the guiding principle, while your value proposition and competitive advantage shape how you interact with your target market and stand out from the competition. These elements form the core of a successful strategy that aligns with your overall business goals and help you achieve sustained growth and success.

Options: Perceptions

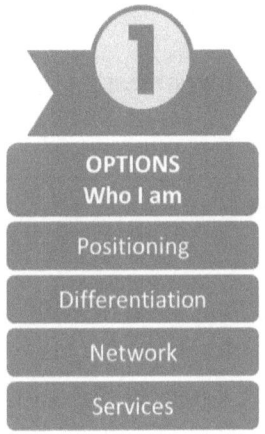

The below paragraph is a specimen questionnaire that helps illustrate your strategic philosophy. It addresses two major things: perception about you and the purpose you have created.

Options	Related Question	Elaboration	Example
Postioning	Where I want to be?	An entrepreneur having my own start-ups, work in large corporations, private equity, where you see yourself in medium and long term future	Corporate - Multi national
Differentiation	Which Specialty?	Finance, medical, sales, law, etc..	Finance
Network	Community - Industry ?	Pharmaceutical, banking, consulting, etc..	Consulting
Services	Career?	General management, operation, finance, etc..	Investment consultant

In this case, the perception created about you is

- Corporate citizen

The purpose you have created is

- Helping people properly manage their investment

Unique value proposition

My value proposition is a direct outcome or a summation of answers to all inquiries related to network relations, network needs, and the penetration strategy. In essence, this forms my unique offering to all my professional stakeholders. I prefer to term this as the W4 proposition. This proposition showcases my distinct capabilities and the value I bring to my professional network, setting me apart from others. It's my unique selling point, demonstrating why I am the best choice in my field.

For instance, if you are an IT consultant, your W4 proposition might be 'Providing innovative, custom-tailored IT solutions that enable businesses to streamline operations and increase efficiency, with a proven record of successful project management and client satisfaction.' This illustrates what you offer, the unique way you provide it, and the benefits your network can expect to gain from it.

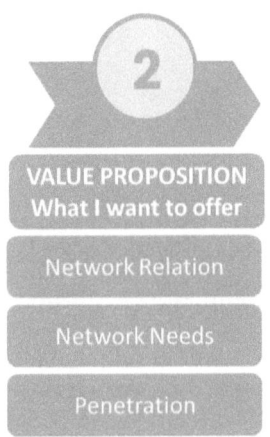

Distinguished Value Proposition

W4 Strategy Framework

The W4 Strategy Framework offers a streamlined approach to crafting your strategy, whether at a personal or business level. It operates on four key questions:

Who Am I?: This question helps you pinpoint your purpose or your organisation's core identity. It delves into understanding your values, passions, and core competencies.

Where Will I Work (Industry & Geography)?: This step involves identifying the context in which you'll operate: the industry and geographic areas where you'll concentrate your efforts. You must consider where your skills or your organisation's competencies are most applicable.

What Will I Offer My Stakeholders?: This focuses on your value proposition: the unique value you will provide to your stakeholders. What problems will you solve, or what needs will you meet?

What Will Be My Added Value, and How Will I Excel in Competition?: This pertains to your competitive advantage: what sets you apart from the competition? How will you differentiate yourself or your organisation in the marketplace?

Once you've successfully addressed these four fundamental W4 questions, you've established the foundation for your strategy. Nevertheless, a robust strategy is not a static document; it must evolve and adapt as circumstances change.

A well-defined value proposition is crucial, characterised by clarity, conciseness, and purpose. To maintain and realise this proposition, you must consistently deliver something competitive to your stakeholders. Ensuring the sustainability of your value proposition entails an ongoing evaluation of your competitive advantage, ensuring that it continues to be relevant and unique in an ever-changing environment.

Competitive advantage

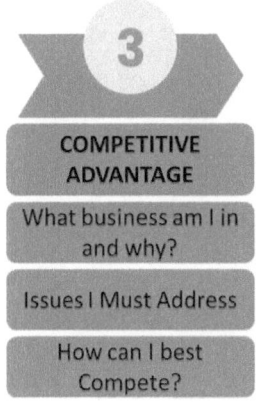

Consider the following three elements when evaluating your competitive advantage:

1. **Business definition:**

    a) Reassess Your Motives: Revisit your reasons for selecting a particular industry or department. Are they still relevant and advantageous?
    b) Explore New Horizons: Be open to horizontal shifts (changing industries or companies) or vertical moves (transitioning to different departments within your current industry or company) as needed.
    c) Define Your Vision, Mission, and Values: Maintain a clear and well-defined vision, mission, and set of

values. These principles should guide your actions and decisions.

d) Fine-Tune Your Value Proposition: Continuously refine your value proposition, ensuring your objectives are SMART (Specific, Measurable, Achievable, Relevant, and Time-bound). This approach helps you maintain focus and direction. The following graphics illustrate these elements:

PHILOSOPHY-DRIVEN STRATEGY

WHAT BUSINESS AM I IN AND WHY?
- Reassess the reason for staying in a certain industry or department?
- Consider moving horizontally (to another industry/company) or vertically (to another department within the same industry/company)
- Clarify your vision, mission, and values
- Keep Specifying your value proposition through SMART objectives (specific, measurable, achievable, relevant, and time-bound)

WHAT ARE THE KEY ISSUES I MUST ADDRESS?
- Listen to feedback, take it seriously, and deal with it with accountability
- Conduct analysis – internal and external to address how best you can improve
- Capitalize on your strength to deal with your areas of development

HOW CAN I BEST COMPETE?
- Stay up to date
- Highlight the differentiating factor in your value proposition? E.g., mobility, adaptability, velocity, education, etc.
- What key activities will enhance the differentiating value proposition?
- What are the technical requirements needed to improve your value proposition? Trainings, qualifications, etc.

2. **To achieve a competitive advantage, you must address the following key points:**

   a) Listen to feedback: Actively listen to feedback from customers, colleagues, and stakeholders. Take their input seriously and be accountable for addressing their concerns.
   b) Conduct analysis: Perform both internal and external analyses to identify areas for improvement. Understand your strengths, weaknesses, opportunities, and threats. This analysis will help you identify the best strategies to enhance your competitive position.
   c) Leverage your strengths: Capitalise on your strengths to address areas of development. Focus on what you do well and use it to overcome challenges and stand out in the market.

3. **How you can best compete:**

   a) Stay up-to-date: Remain informed about industry trends, market changes, and advancements in your field. Continuous learning and staying updated will keep you competitive and relevant.
   b) Highlight differentiating factors: Identify the unique aspects of your value proposition that set you apart from competitors. This could be your mobility, adaptability, velocity, specialised education, or any other distinct features that appeal to your target audience.

c) Enhance value proposition through key activities: Determine the specific activities that can strengthen your value proposition further. This could include enhancing customer service, optimising production processes, or improving marketing strategies.

d) Invest in technical requirements: Assess the technical skills and qualifications required to improve your value proposition. Invest in necessary training, certifications, or qualifications to enhance your capabilities and maintain a competitive edge.

By addressing these points, you will be better positioned to compete effectively and maintain a strong competitive advantage in your industry or market.

Conclusion

In this chapter, the significance of philosophy driving strategy is discussed. I highlighted the imperative role of strategy, the roadmap that guides us toward our objectives, regardless of the circumstances or stages of our lives.

Just as corporations rely on guiding philosophies to shape their strategies, individuals, too, should cultivate personal philosophies that govern their life's decisions. I strongly encourage you to ponder the questions presented, fearlessly adding more, that align with your unique life circumstances.

10

CONCLUSION

The central aim of this book is to inspire readers to embrace and integrate the following eight transformative steps into their personal and professional lives:

Step 1: Success involves a comprehensive journey, intertwining technical skills with positive behaviors. Keep in mind the "Future Success Equation" to recall how ambitions align with your capabilities. (Refer to, in Chapter 2)

Step 2: Develop the ability to make prudent decisions by effectively setting priorities (detailed in Chapter 3).

Step 3: Cultivate dynamic leadership qualities that inspire and motivate those around you (explored in Chapter 4).

Step 4: Continuous productivity: Remember that past achievements are not resting laurels, avoid succumbing to the leaders' derailment syndrome (discussed in Chapter 5).

Step 5: Remain current and highly skilled in your chosen field, maintaining a commitment to lifelong learning (highlighted in Chapter 6).

Step 6: Foster a culture of respect and love in all your interactions, always prepared to take the first step (expounded upon in Chapter 7).

Step 7: Understand the art of healthy competition and learn to appreciate your competitors (uncovered in Chapter 8).

Step 8: Ensure that your life's direction is guided by a well-defined, meaningful philosophy (elucidated in Chapter 9).

Through these steps, I aspire to help you create a fulfilling, successful life both personally and professionally.

AUTHOR BIO

Abboud serves as the CEO of GEN Business Partner for Aspire Group, a California-based company for the Middle East and CIS region. Additionally, he is a Managing Partner for the Health & Life Care Science division of Infomed, a board member of Julphar Pharmaceutical, Chair of its Nomination and Remuneration Committee, and a member of the Strategic and Technical Committee. He is certified as a consultant for numerous multinational healthcare consultancy firms, including Guidepoint, GLG, and Atheneum Consultation. His leadership extends to co-heading the Harvard HealthCare Association's Middle East Chapter.

His extensive experience as a Vice President, Board of Directors Member, and Senior Consultant in the healthcare industry is complemented by a track record of high achievements in the pharmaceutical sector. Until 2018, Abboud served as a Vice President at AbbVie, overseeing the Middle East and Africa Region operations and held the chairmanship of the PhRMA association, where he enacted a major restructure. Earlier in his career, Abboud was a Regional Director MENA at Abbott and worked in Financial Consulting at Arthur Anderson.

Abboud holds an Advanced Management Programme (AMP) from Harvard Business School, a Master's Degree in Finance from St Joseph University, and has attended executive programs at prestigious institutions such as INSEAD, University of Barcelona, and Case Western University. Abboud is a certified International Management Accountant (IMA) – New Jersey Board.

Fluent in Arabic, English, and French, Abboud brings vast international experience, having lived and worked in numerous countries, including the USA, Canada, Greece, Kuwait, Dubai, Saudi Arabia, and Lebanon.

Significant Achievements:

- Board member and consultant to regional pharmaceutical companies, guiding them through restructuring and operational optimization.
- Consultant to large investment companies, advising on their healthcare investments.
- Implementation of expert supply chain processes, from forecasting to manufacturing.

- Management of several regional medical associations and active participation in important regional disease awareness campaigns.
- Reformation of the Pharmaceutical Industry Association in the Middle East and Africa.
- Consultation with several regional governments on healthcare policy strategy and international investment attraction, including working with the Egyptian government in the fight to eradicate HCV.
- Enhanced the regional investments of his company by recognizing and harnessing the Middle East's growth potential, resulting in a robust Abbott/Abbvie presence in the region.
- Launched multiple therapeutic areas, including HCV, Immunology, and Oncology.
- Pioneered the establishment of third-party manufacturing with partners across the MEA Region, including Saudi Arabia and Egypt.
- Established and structured Abbott and Abbvie regional offices to align with commercial needs, built strategic partnerships with robust agents, and achieved a high record of 35 per cent CGR sales growth.
- Led the global implementation of the Sarbanes-Oxley Act (Expenses section) across Abbott following the 2008 economic crisis.

Abboud's career has been decorated with multiple awards, including the three-time receipt of the Numero Uno top achiever and Company Global Change Agent during his tenure at Abbott and Abbvie. Recently, he was honored with the Healthcare Excellence Award from Health2.0-2023 for his exceptional achievements in the Middle East Region.

In addition to his professional accomplishments, Abboud is deeply committed to social responsibility. He serves as the chairman of the Don Bosco Culture Centre, a non-governmental organization dedicated to empowering youth and vulnerable individuals, enhancing their capabilities and capacities. Furthermore, Abboud holds a position as a board member at "Maison Du Futur," a prominent think tank organization in the Middle East region. Through these roles, he actively contributes to initiatives that uplift and support communities, demonstrating his dedication to making a positive impact beyond the corporate realm.

Stay in touch

LinkedIn: www.linkedin.com/in/abboud-bejjani-
email: abboud.bejjani@infomedweb.com
Tel: +971504511816

Notes

www.ingramcontent.com/pod-product-compliance
Lightning Source LLC
Chambersburg PA
CBHW021104080526
44587CB00010B/377